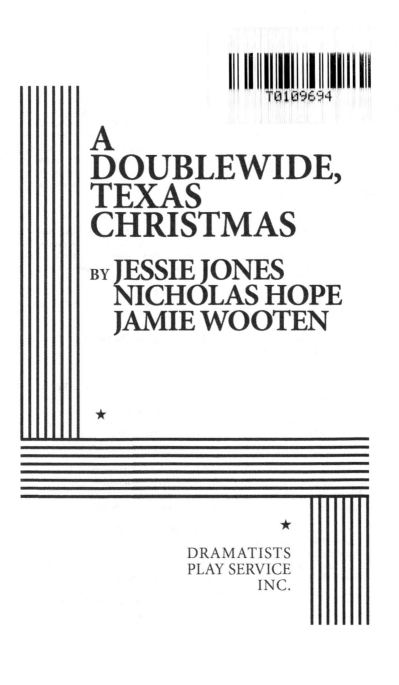

A DOUBLEWIDE, TEXAS CHRISTMAS

BY JESSIE JONES
NICHOLAS HOPE
JAMIE WOOTEN

★

DRAMATISTS
PLAY SERVICE
INC.

A DOUBLEWIDE, TEXAS CHRISTMAS
Copyright © 2018, Jessie Jones, Nicholas Hope, Jamie Wooten

2

A DOUBLEWIDE, TEXAS CHRISTMAS received its world premiere at Theatre Off The Square in Weatherford, Texas, on December 1, 2017. It was directed by Jon R. Kruse; the assistant directors were Roberta Furman, Chuck Hudson, and Wally Jones; the stage manager was Jessica Michel; the lighting design was by Wally Jones and Jesse James; the set design was by Chuck Hudson; the sound design was by Nikolai Braswell; the costume design was by Jessica Michel and Peggy Osburn; the property design was by Jessica Michel and Linda Hudson; the original Jones Hope Wooten show logo was designed by Joe Connor and Mike Stevens. The cast was as follows:

BIG ETHEL SATTERWHITE .... Debra Gass
GEORGIA DEAN RUDD .... Rebecca Young
LARK BARKEN .... Kate Cowling
HAYWOOD SLOGGETT .... Dan Parris
PATSY PRICE .... Kathy Manning
NORWAYNE "BABY" CRUMPLER .... Ray Shannon
JOVEETA CRUMPLER .... Megan Hamilton
CAPRICE CRUMPLER .... Peggy Osburn
NASH SLOGGETT .... Nikolai Braswell

AUTHORS' NOTES

We suggest up-tempo Christmas music be played pre- and post-show, at intermission, and especially during scene transitions.

We urge scene changes be made as quickly as possible to maintain a lively pace for the play, especially in Act Two between Scenes 5 and 6.

The actor who portrays Nash can also provide the voice of Harley.

A lifelike doll should portray the "role" of Arden Rose.

The flyers Lark passes out to the audience in Act Two, Scene 1, should be printed with promotional information for relocation to Doublewide.

CHARACTERS

BIG ETHEL SATTERWHITE, 60s

GEORGIA DEAN RUDD, 40s

LARK BARKEN, 20s

HAYWOOD SLOGGETT, 70s

PATSY PRICE, 60s

NORWAYNE "BABY" CRUMPLER, 40s

JOVEETA CRUMPLER, 40s

CAPRICE CRUMPLER, 70s

NASH SLOGGETT, 40s

HARLEY DOBBS, 40s (Voiceover Only)

PLACE

In and around the living room of Joveeta's mobile home in the trailer park community of Doublewide, Texas. Other locations are indicated by pools of light.

TIME

The present.
The action of the play takes place over two weeks in December leading up to Christmas.

A DOUBLEWIDE, TEXAS CHRISTMAS

ACT ONE

Scene 1

A spotlight comes up downstage center on a lectern. Big Ethel Satterwhite, brusque, down-to-earth, enters stage right in colorful nurse's scrubs, stethoscope around her neck, carries a flashlight, strides to the lectern, addresses the audience.

BIG ETHEL. Well, this is a real good turnout. And I don't care what anybody says, y'all clean up right nice. I want to thank all you residents here at Stairway to Heaven Retirement Village for comin' out to participate in this afternoon's Senior Seminar: "Holiday Buffets—Good Eats or Deathtrap On A Plate?" And for those with short-term memory challenges, let me remind you that I'm Big Ethel Satterwhite, the L.V.N. on duty. Now, with Christmas bearin' down on us, we know full well that your guilt-riddled family members are gonna take you out and wine and dine you so you'll forget you haven't seen 'em in six months. But when you get to your trashy daughter-in-law's house—the one who's got her eye on the family silver—you'll be faced with gooey pies, bowls of congealed mess and platters of Southern-fried artery clog guaranteed to stroke you out by New Year's. Now, if you show a little dietary restraint, you'll have a fair shot at makin' it 'til Easter. You might even live long enough to see your son realize the error of his ways and give that skank the boot! And speakin' of buffets, the folks at the Tabernacle of the Lamb will be sharin' some Yuletide goodies with us when we caravan over to Fayro in two weeks to attend their annual Christmas Program. And if anyone spots a dish of Sissy Fowler's Dreamy Potted Meat Thumb Rolls, give us a heads up. We can't afford a repeat of the gastrointestinal upset we all endured in the van comin' home from last year's festivities. *(Fans the air.)* Not that I'm mentionin' any names, *Orlene Plunkett!* And that's our official discussion for today. *(Makes sure no other staff members are around. Then, low.)* Now, let's get down to business. Speakin' of *sharin' your goodies*, as the staff medical professional, it's my job to make sure y'all are all enjoyin' a good life. But some of you may be enjoyin' yourselves a little too much. A pair of boxer shorts and a peek-a-boo negligee were found hangin' from the azaleas out by the fish pond. And those are not the first unmentionables found scattered around the property. People, thrashin' through the bushes fueled by raw lust could have dire consequences, especially on a frosty mornin'. Look, everyone loves a little *slap and tickle* now and again. For example, I tolerate a little kiss and a wink from my husband, O.C., once every seven or eight months or so whether I like it or not. Perfectly healthy and even— *(Her attention caught, shines the flashlight on an audience member.)* Now *this* is exactly what I'm talkin' about. Chubby Tate, you keep them wanderin' hands *off* Miss Inetta! *(Snaps off the flashlight.)* I know everyone here at Stairway to Heaven wants to go out with a smile on your face, but if you people keep this up, y'all may be climbin' them stairs a lot sooner than you counted on. So find yourself some other activities—jog on the treadmill, learn to knit. Or better yet, somebody *please* finish that tacky Thomas Kinkade jigsaw puzzle in the rec room. *(Sighs.)* But if you're hell-bent on *makin' those bells on bobtails ring*, for the love of Mike, have the decency to stay in your room and lock the door. 'Cause frankly, the less chance one of us staff members has of seein' *you* rockin' around the Christmas tree, the better *our* chances are of sleepin' in heavenly peace! *(Blackout.)*

Scene 2

Later that afternoon. A spotlight comes up downstage left on a bench and a coat rack with a couple of coats hanging on it nearby—the storeroom of Bronco Betty's Buffeteria. Georgia Dean Rudd, gregarious ball of fire, hurries in stage left in jeans, ruffled shirt, fringed apron, cowboy hat, big earrings, neck scarf, all in her signature color, hot pink. Talks on her phone.

GEORGIA DEAN. …Ozella Smoot, I understand y'all are busy there at the hospital, we're swamped here at the Buffeteria, too— today's lunch rush almost did us in. But I need to know how Earlcody is doing since they hauled him off this morning… *What?! Another* stent? That's got to put him into double digits. Y'all trying to meet a year-end sales quota or something?… Yeah, he collapsed serving up the Smokers Anonymous prayer breakfast. Seeing him face down in the grits upset those weak sisters so bad they all raced outside and sucked down a pack of Camels… Listen, Lark and I are on our way… I don't give a flip about I.C.U. rules, I've worked for Earlcody here at Bronco Betty's since I was sixteen so I *will* get in to see him… What?! That's blackmail… Okay, fine. If he's still got a pulse when we show up, I'll have a bear claw with your name on it. *(Hangs up, as Lark, a guileless, bespectacled young woman in an identical uniform, enters stage left.)*

LARK. Sorry it took so long to bus the tables, Georgia Dean, but half of McTwayne County must've eaten lunch here today. The bottomless banana pudding promotion you came up with is really packing them in.

GEORGIA DEAN. *(Removes her apron.)* Yeah, but I doubt we made a profit today, Lark. Once Dessie Murch waddled in here, I knew it would take a cattle prod to get her away from the trough. I swear I saw sparks flying off her spoon.

LARK. I'm so glad we're closing early to go see Earlcody. I know you've been after him to eat healthier. *(Quickly removes her apron.)*

And in his defense, he *did* put a leaf of lettuce on his double cheese-burger yesterday.

GEORGIA DEAN. That won't cut it. He needs to clean up his act. Earlcody's promised the buffeteria is all mine when he retires, but I don't like walking around thinking I'm just one chicken-fried steak away from owning this joint.

LARK. I know you worry about that sweet old man, but when you *do* take over this place, it'll be awesome. That's bound to be a dream-come-true for you.

GEORGIA DEAN. Yes, ma'am. I'm finally inching up on happiness. I love my work, my home, my friends, I've got it all. *(Grabs both their coats.)* And it only took surviving forty-five-plus years, ditching two deadbeat husbands and cultivating a natural talent for thrifty and dramatic accessorizing to make it happen.

LARK. I'm finding my bliss, too. In fact, my aura has been pre-dominantly orange for a while now. You gave me this job, then I met everyone in Doublewide and had my baby. And with the little excep-tion of losing my new husband in that tragic sky-diving accident, it's been a really great year.

GEORGIA DEAN. And I swear this coming year will be even better.

LARK. Hey, it's almost Christmas, maybe Santa will bring you Mr. Wonderful.

GEORGIA DEAN. At this point I'd settle for Mr. Good-Enough-In-A-Pinch or, heck, during a *really* lonely stretch, I'd take Mr. Finally-Working-A-Job-And-Hasn't-Violated-Parole. *(Sighs.)* No, the last Mr. Wonderful in my life was your daddy. But Nash Sloggett was the one who got away. *(They put on their coats.)*

LARK. He got away from me, too—never even knew I was born. But I'd sure love to know him and let him meet his granddaughter and see the people who've been so good to me since I came here from Oregon. That's my Christmas wish.

GEORGIA DEAN. That's a good one. And *mine* is the same thing every woman over forty wishes for—one good cycle through the clothes dryer. *(Off Lark's puzzled look.)* 'Cause then we'd come out wrinkle-free and two sizes smaller! *(They laugh and exit stage left. Blackout.)*

Scene 3

An hour later. Lights up downstage center on a large, plastic illuminated nativity figure. Haywood Sloggett, a spry, older man in khakis and cardigan with a sleeping six-month-old baby in a snuggly enters stage right. He's giving his sister, Patsy Price, a former society matron in a dated designer suit, a tour.

SLOGGETT. *(Points.)* …And this here is the town hall of Double-wide, Texas. Planted those shrubs around the steps myself.

PATSY. *(Looks around.)* Ugh. Four trailers and a shed. All that's missing from this little piece of paradise is a couple of tumbleweeds and a chainsaw murderer.

SLOGGETT. You have got to change that attitude. This is your new home, your chance to start a new life, little sister. Make friends, find something that makes you happy. 'Cause right now you're about as much fun as a case of shingles.

PATSY. *(Sarcastic.)* You are so right, I should be jumping for joy. My brother took me in because I have nowhere else to go. *Me* who devoted my entire adult life to charitable works. And yet those cretins just across the county in Fayro turned against me. Even my own son, Parker, and his hateful wife, Tina Jo, denounced me. Then I got hoodwinked out of all my money *and* on my last birthday it hit me that in dog years I'm *dead*. So, yeah, I should be *ecstatic!*

SLOGGETT. Don't rewrite history, Patsy. *You* did all this. You whipped up so much drama Parker and Tina Jo couldn't take it anymore. The pity party is over.

PATSY. Not as long as I'm stuck out here in Buzzard Gulch.

SLOGGETT. Our brand-new town might be your last shot. After my wife died, I was eat up with loneliness—I was miserable and mean. But the people here forgave my rotten behavior and gave me my life back. The same could happen for you…if you try. Trust me, these folks are kind and generous and smart. *(Norwayne "Baby" Crumpler, enthusiastic good ol' boy in a flannel shirt and vest, cut-off camouflage pants, work boots, enters downstage left, drags two long*

11

strings of unlit Christmas lights—"plugged in" offstage—behind him, one in each hand.)

BABY. Countdown to Christmas, Mr. Sloggett! Santy Claus is makin' his list and checkin' it twice! Mama had me wire a wreath to the grille of that broke-down pickup in front of our trailer. I think it really dresses up the place, don't you? Oh, and Mama made you a batch of fudge to apologize for flashin' you this mornin' when she crawled up on the roof to fix the satellite dish. She heard you scream when the wind blew her robe open and she's real sorry.

SLOGGETT. Not as sorry as I was. What has she got against wearing underwear?

PATSY. *(Dry.)* And life in the holler just keeps getting better and better.

BABY. *(Whispers.)* I didn't know little Arden Rose was asleep. That's good 'cause I'm decoratin' the town for her first Christmas. I got these lights real cheap over in Tugaloo. *(Plugs them together, SFX: Loud, electrical buzz. He's hit with a long electric jolt. He shakes and shudders a few beats, pulls them apart.)* Now I know why.

PATSY. *(To Sloggett.)* One of your resident rocket scientists? *(He glares at her.)* What? I wasn't insulting his intelligence, I was saluting his stupidity.

BABY. *(Sincere.)* Why, thank you. *(Then.)* You gotta excuse my manners, ma'am. I'm Norwayne Crumpler, but everyone calls me Baby.

SLOGGETT. Yep, he's Chief of Police *and* heads up the fire department, 'course that just means he knows where the hose is. But Baby keeps this town moving.

BABY. Sure do. I'm also in charge of cleanin' the town's septic tanks. *(Sticks out his hand.)* Put 'er there. *(Patsy recoils.)*

SLOGGETT. *(Quickly covers.)* Uh, this is my sister. She's going to be living with us here in Doublewide over at my house.

BABY. Boy howdy! Talk about a red-letter day! I hear we've got *another* new resident movin' in, too, but Mama says *she's* big time trouble straight from the funny farm. So we're extra glad to have you, Ms. Sloggett. You seem real nice.

12

SLOGGETT. *(Quickly.)* Baby, I ought to—

BABY. *(On a roll.)* Yeah, that other woman's named Patsy Price and she used to live in Fayro, but evidently she's a real snot pot and mean as a snake.

SLOGGETT. Baby, what you need to know is that—

BABY. *(Oblivious.)* Here's a funny story—few years back, that Patsy took pain pills she thought were aspirin right before the Christmas pageant and got so messed up she made a Class-A jackass of herself right there in the Tabernacle of the Lamb. Wish I coulda seen it. Everyone in town had a good laugh at her expense and it gave that Ms. Price such a nervous breakdown it landed her smack-dab in the looney bin. *(Laughs heartily.)* Some people sure are idiots, right?

PATSY. No argument there. And F.Y.I., *I'm* Patsy Price. Patsy *Sloggett* Price.

BABY. *(Slowly stops laughing.)* Oops. Guess I really stepped in it, huh?

SLOGGETT. Yep. I'd say about knee deep this time.

BABY. You know…maybe I'll do less talkin' and more decoratin'. Gotta go get these lights fixed. *(Picks up the strings of lights.)*

PATSY. *(Desperate.)* And waste a perfectly good electrical current?! Give me those things! It's my way out of here! *(Grabs the lights. Slams the plugs together, SFX: Loud, electrical buzz, she's hit with an electric jolt, shakes and shudders dramatically a few seconds. Sloggett and Baby look on in horror.)*

BABY. Ms. Patsy! Don't hold on to— *(Suddenly, all the Christmas lights come on. Patsy stops vibrating. Baby and Sloggett are delighted, forget about her.)* Hey, you fixed 'em! Right neighborly of you. *(To Sloggett.)* She might be mean *and* crazy, but she'll fit in just fine. *(Back to her.)* Merry Christmas, Ms. Patsy. And welcome to Doublewide! *(She shakes and shudders dramatically one more time. Blackout.)*

Scene 4

*Later that afternoon. Lights up downstage right on two bar
stools. A sheaf of papers is on one, a cell phone on the other
rings as Caprice Crumpler, an older woman battling age
and losing the fight, dressed in form-fitting clothes much too
young for her age, saunters in stage right with a beer bottle.
SFX: Laughter and glasses clinking are heard in the back-
ground as she answers the phone.*

CAPRICE. You got Caprice Crumpler—doesn't get much better than
that. What can I do you for?... Uh, hold a sec. *(Covers phone, yells off
stage right.)* Y'all pipe down! My bossy daughter's checking up on me.
And Pug Hoover, get your sorry butt off my stool! Everyone knows *I*
sit under the Lone Star Beer clock! *(Into phone, sweet.)* Hello, Shug...
Well, you *can't* have been trying to reach me for an hour, I'm right
here at the courthouse. This place is so quiet I would've heard the
phone ring... Why do you always jump to that? What kind of mother
would spend *all* her time at some bar like the Stagger Inn? *(Unseen by
Caprice, Joveeta Crumpler, dressed in a jacket and jeans, phone to her
ear, enters stage left, slowly makes her way to Caprice.)* I'll have you
know, I'm a patriotic Texan, I take my civic responsibilities seriously.
(Makes a dramatic gesture, beer bottle in hand.) Yes, as I gaze around
this historic courthouse, this seat of democracy, I am filled with pride
that we've started our own town and I believe down to the very bot-
tom of my heart that... *(Turns, sees Joveeta.)* I am dead meat.

JOVEETA. And as *I* gaze around this bar, this seat of *debauchery*,
I'm filled with shock and awe that a beer and a good time mean
more to you than your daughter.

CAPRICE. Joveeta, they do *not* mean more to me...they mean *as
much* to me, but definitely not more.

JOVEETA. Mama, our town meeting tonight is important! Our
brand new little town is struggling to survive. We need that info
from the courthouse to make sure we asked for the right grants.
You blew it! It's after five. County offices are closed.

CAPRICE. Oh, ye of little faith and even less fashion sense. *(Hands over the papers.)* I got your figures. I only stopped by here to sign a few autographs for my fans. When you're a star, it's expected of you. Celebrity has its responsibilities.

JOVEETA. *(Studies the papers.)* Look, you are not a celebrity, you're a woman on Social Security living in a trailer in a town with a population of *ten.* And four cable access commercials for Jarvis Womble's Funeral Home *do not* make you a "celebrity." Come on, how much popularity can playing a *corpse* generate?

CAPRICE. Plenty! I get fan mail! And I'll have you know that Elvis' estate has made way more money since he *died* than it did when he was *alive.* So don't you be putting down the power of a *celebrity corpse.*

JOVEETA. *(At wit's end.)* Let's talk about this later. I'm taking you home.

CAPRICE. Girl, you are in a bad way. You're tense, always on edge. Now I didn't want to give you this 'til Christmas, but that's two weeks away, and you need it now. *(Rummages in her bra, pulls out an envelope, hands it to her.)* Merry Christmas and you're welcome. *(Joveeta, resigned, reluctantly opens it.)*

JOVEETA. *(Pulls out a card.)* A gift card for a singles' match-up service? Really?

CAPRICE. It's for lonely women over forty who think all hope is gone.

JOVEETA. *(Reads.) Desperate Times, Desperate Measures Dating Club?!*

CAPRICE. Yes, and if that doesn't say *Joveeta Crumpler*, nothing does. Now, the membership expires New Year's Eve—that's why I got it so cheap, so hop on it. It's your last on-ramp to the freeway of love. You've only got three weeks to find your soul mate…or at least trick some poor old, broke-down fool into believing—

JOVEETA. Mama, I'm the mayor of Doublewide. I gave up my career to start the town from scratch. I'm living in a trailer that is also our town hall which results in zero privacy. All I do is work and try to keep you out of this bar. What on earth would I do with a man?!

CAPRICE. See! That's it right there! The fact that you even have to *ask* what to do with a man is *exactly why* you need this membership. Now get on it and I'll just go back to my fans. *(Starts to cross away, Joveeta grabs her arm.)*

15

JOVEETA. Oh, no you don't. Listen to me, you old barfly. We're leaving and when we get home, you're helping me set up for the meeting. It starts at six-thirty.

CAPRICE. Alright, alright! Keep your shirt on, party-pooper! But if my fan mail falls off, *it is on your head. (Stomps out, stage left.)*

JOVEETA. *(Sighs, looks up into the light.)* Santa, all I want for Christmas is a mother who's *normal.* Is that too much to ask? *(Caprice hurries back in.)*

CAPRICE. Listen, we need to stop by the Funeral Home. Jarvis got in a new casket this morning and I promised to give it a test drive. *(Rushes out stage left.)*

JOVEETA. *(Continues to look into the light.)* Okay, if *that's* out, how about a pair of Spanx? *(Blackout.)*

Scene 5

That night. Lights come up on the well-worn living room of Joveeta's doublewide that is also Town Hall. Upstage center is the front door, a window on one side. A dinette table is in front of the window. On the stage right wall is a hall doorway that leads to bedrooms, bathroom and back door. On the stage left wall is a swinging door to the kitchen. Downstage from that is a desk, a chair and a Texas and American flag standing on either side. An old sofa is downstage right. Left of the sofa is an easy chair. Joveeta hurriedly rakes makeup and personal items into the desk drawers. Georgia Dean enters from hall with two folding chairs.

GEORGIA DEAN. *(Places the chairs.)* So, Madam Mayor, are you ready for tonight?

JOVEETA. We'll see. Look, I need some advice. Do you—

GEORGIA DEAN. I thought you'd never ask! Rethink your hairstyle, pluck those eyebrows and for heaven's sake, Shug, burn *everything* in that closet of yours. I mean, a girl *deserves* to update her wardrobe every couple of decades or so.

JOVEETA. That's…not where I was headed, but good to know. Actually, *(Takes out a card.)* Mama gave me a dating club gift card. I don't know what to do with it.

GEORGIA DEAN. Use it! *(Takes it, reads.)* "Desperate Times, Desperate Measures"? If that doesn't scream "Joveeta Crumpler," nothing does.

JOVEETA. *(Snatches back the card.)* Why does everyone keep saying that?!

GEORGIA DEAN. Shoot, if you're not going to use it, I will.

JOVEETA. Fine. *(Tosses it onto desk.)* You're more excited about it and *clearly* I don't have the *wardrobe* for it. And may that limited-time membership bring you good tidings of great joy.

GEORGIA DEAN. Huh. Not really feeling the urge to deck the halls yet, are you?

JOVEETA. It's just all this town business. For some reason, we still haven't gotten our final official incorporation papers and I've waited months to find out what grants we qualify for. We need them to pave the road, get a sidewalk…the list is endless. But I can't get any answers from the County Commissioners and— *(Caprice enters from hall doorway with Arden Rose.)*

CAPRICE. Girl, how many times do I have to tell you—when you're dealing with the government, don't get mad, get ugly.

JOVEETA. And it's *that* kind of folk wisdom that's red-flagged you for a tax audit every year since Moses wore diapers. So why aren't you in the kitchen helping instead of playing with Arden Rose?

CAPRICE. Because Lark had one of her brainstorms. *(Low.)* Forget tasty snacks. It's healthy glorp for everyone. It's your fault, Georgia Dean—you and all them yams.

GEORGIA DEAN. They sent an extra crate to Bronco Betty's and I'm not going to waste good food. I even took some to Earlcody's nurses.

CAPRICE. Yeah, well one bite of Lark's Yammy Tofu Nauseators and you'll sing another tune. *(Coos to the baby.)* I love you and wouldn't feed you that crap. And you love me. Say *Caprice*. Come on, say it—*Ca-price*. *(Joveeta and Georgia Dean go to her.)*

GEORGIA DEAN. That's so selfish, trying to get her to say your

17

name first. Since we live together, I'm like a grandma to her, naturally her first words will be *(Coos to the baby.)* Geor-gia Dean. *Geor-gia Dean.*

JOVEETA. I help Sloggett take care of her during the day. The first thing she says might well be *(Coos.)* Jo-vee-ta. Say, *Jo-vee-ta.*

CAPRICE. You two stay out of this. *(To the baby.)* Ca-price. Let me hear it. *(All three coo their names to the baby as Lark enters, unnoticed, from the kitchen.)*

LARK. No offense, but I hope her first word is *Mama.*

CAPRICE. *(Embarrassed.)* Oh, yeah. Well, we meant *after* that. Right, girls? *(Sheepish, Joveeta and Georgia Dean cover, nod in agreement.)*

LARK. Yeah, I thought so. *(Takes the baby.)* Come on, Peanut. *(Sees the dating club card, picks it up, reads.)* "Desperate Times, Desperate Measures Dating Club." Oh, how perfect! Joveeta, it's got your name all over it. *(Puts it on the desk, exits through hall doorway.)*

JOVEETA. For Pete's sake! Did y'all take a vote on this or something?! *(Sloggett sticks his head in front door.)*

SLOGGETT. Hope we're not early. Caprice, is that you? After seeing so much of you swinging in the breeze this morning, I hardly recognized you with clothes *on.*

CAPRICE. Just doing my part to keep Texas beautiful, old man. You could do *yours* by moving to Arkansas.

SLOGGETT. Anyway, we're here for the meeting. I brought my sister with me.

GEORGIA DEAN. Patsy just moved in. Is she up for this tonight?

SLOGGETT. Oh, yeah. She *really wants* to be here. Wild horses couldn't keep her away. *(Enters, tugs Patsy in by a rope he's lassoed around her.)*

PATSY. *(Flat, disingenuous.)* I can't tell you how thrilled I am to be here.

CAPRICE. About as thrilled as we are to be stuck with you. Take a seat. I'm sure moving in and maintaining that superiority complex must have you exhausted. *(Exits into the kitchen.)*

JOVEETA. Which is just Mama's way of saying "welcome to the

neighborhood." *(She unties Patsy, drops rope by the couch.)* This is Town Hall, it's also my home.

SLOGGETT. It was Georgia Dean's Aunt Minona's trailer. Big gal, big heart.

GEORGIA DEAN. You betcha. Five hundred and twenty pounds of goodness. After she passed, the paramedics renamed the hydraulic winch they used to lift her out of here—The Mighty Minona. I just tear up every time I think about that.

PATSY. I have died and gone to hell. *(Plops in the middle of the sofa which is so broken down, she sinks all the way to the floor, her knees level with her head.)* I'm guessing this was Minona's favorite spot. *(Sloggett and Georgia Dean hurry to pull her out of the deep dip. Baby flings open front door, looks in.)*

BABY. Georgia Dean, I'm tryin' to move those baby raccoons out of that old Kenmore at the side of your trailer. Where do you want 'em?

GEORGIA DEAN. Baby, you know better than to mess with those raccoons.

BABY. No, they're sweet and the big one really likes me. She— *(Just then, a raccoon attacks Baby's neck [i.e., a life-sized stuffed toy is tossed at Baby's head by an unseen stagehand]. Baby screams, grapples with the raccoon, they both disappear from view. Georgia Dean lets go of Patsy, who falls back into the sofa.)*

GEORGIA DEAN. *(Calls.)* Baby, I told you not to hang Christmas lights on that stove! Raccoons don't give a hoot about the holidays! *(Exits front door. Joveeta and Sloggett pull Patsy out.)*

PATSY. Oh, please let a twister come and take me away from all this! *(Lark enters from hall doorway.)*

LARK. Great-Aunt Patsy! I am so glad you're here. *(Hugs her.)* Can I get you something to drink?

PATSY. How about some eggnog with a side of strychnine? *(Lark laughs.)*

LARK. I'll go check on my snacks. Hope you like yams. *(Exits into kitchen.)*

SLOGGETT. *(Low, to Patsy.)* Is she the spitting image of Nash or what? And don't mention this, but I'm trying to locate my boy and get him home for the holidays. Maybe he's forgiven me for the past. Anyway, that's Lark's Christmas wish and I want to make it come true.

PATSY. What a great idea, 'cause nothing says "Merry Christmas" better than digging up and airing out sad, old family secrets.

SLOGGETT. *(Oblivious.)* Great! I knew you'd be on board. *(Caprice enters from the kitchen with a bottle of beer. SFX: Animal growls and screeches! CRASH!)*

CAPRICE. What the Sam Hill is going on outside? *(Georgia Dean and Baby race in front door, slam it, stand against it to secure it.)*

GEORGIA DEAN. A herd of raccoons is attacking the trailer! I *told* Baby not to stir 'em up! As long as we stay inside, we're safe. *(Unnoticed, Patsy loops Sloggett's rope around her neck, lifts it as if hanging herself. Sloggett swipes it out of her hand, glares.)*

JOVEETA. Okay, enough *Wild Kingdom. (Goes to the desk, raps a small gavel on a sound block several times. Lark hurries in from the kitchen.)* We'll have to start without Big Ethel and O.C. Take a seat, folks. *(They do, avoiding the middle of the sofa.)* Thanks for coming. I know we're all busy right before Christmas.

CAPRICE. Especially if you're a celebrity—everyone wants to see you, get an autograph, it's enough to drive a woman to drink. *(Knocks back a slug of beer.)*

JOVEETA. Uh-huh. *(Goes on.)* Now it was hard keeping the City of Tugaloo from annexing our trailer park which is exactly why we incorporated Doublewide as its own town and—

CAPRICE. Old news!

JOVEETA. *(Annoyed.)* Yes, but our *new* resident doesn't know the story.

PATSY. The new resident doesn't really care.

LARK. Oh, you will. You'll fall in love with Doublewide just like I did.

PATSY. I might. I might also wake up tomorrow morning lying next to Brad Pitt. I'd say the odds are about the same.

JOVEETA. O-kay, let's stay focused. As you know, we've applied for county grants and we're waiting for the Board of— *(Big Ethel hurries in hall doorway, breathless.)*

BIG ETHEL. A pack of raccoons just ambushed me on the front

porch! I barely made it to the back door. Like I needed that! The second I got home, O.C. started in on my bein' gone so much. He snapped, "You promised you'd spend your whole life tryin' to make me happy." I said, "Yeah, but I never expected you to live this long!"

CAPRICE. So where is O.C.? Isn't he coming?

BIG ETHEL. Not as long as there's a game on, and there's *always* a game on. I chalk O.C. not showin' up to bein' just another one of his boneheaded decisions.

GEORGIA DEAN. Careful, Big Ethel. Never make fun of your husband's choices. Remember, *you're one of 'em. (The others laugh.)*

JOVEETA. *(Annoyed, raps the gavel.)* Okay, folks, town business is no laughing matter. Let's get back to it. *(Raps the gavel.)* Remember, the mayor's got the gavel.

BIG ETHEL. *(Grabs gavel.)* And now the town L.V.N. has it. I've got big news.

JOVEETA. This is *my* meeting and that is *my* gavel. *(Tries to grab it, fails.)*

BIG ETHEL. Well, it's mine now and I don't see another one any-where else. So listen up! I just heard that on Christmas Eve, in Fayro, on the lawn of the Tabernacle of the Lamb, instead of the *usual* program, there'll be a competition to see which town has the most creative and ingenious reimaginin' of that big night in Bethlehem. It's called *Battle of the Mangers.* Every town in McTwayne County has entered—Tugaloo, Fayro, Sweetgum, even Tinsel. They're all set to compete *but have completely ignored us. (Joveeta grabs at the gavel, Big Ethel keeps it.)*

CAPRICE. They can't do that! We're a town now, too…or *will* be when we get those incorporation papers. We can't let them disrespect us! *(Frustrated, Joveeta hurries out hall doorway.)*

BIG ETHEL. Agreed! So I signed us up. Doublewide is officially entered to compete against the other towns. And we *will* win this Nativity Smackdown. But we're at a disadvantage—the other towns have been workin' on it for a while.

LARK. That only gives us two weeks. First we need a theme, some-thing flashy.

GEORGIA DEAN. Disco! I'm seein' mirror balls, glitz and Mary in palazzo pants, Joseph in platform shoes. We can call it… *(Idea!)* "O Holy Night Fever"!

BIG ETHEL. *(Beat.)* Um…*I'll* come up with somethin'.

SLOGGETT. I'm in! *(Pointedly.)* Patsy, don't *you* want to throw yourself into it?

PATSY. Not as much as I want to throw myself off a bridge right now.

BIG ETHEL. Well, nobody would fault you since your daughter-in-law *is* headin' up the whole shebang.

BABY. Yeah, everybody knows there's bad blood between you and Tina Jo.

PATSY. *(Snaps to attention.)* Tina Jo? She's in charge of the event?

LARK. Well, I think it's okay if you really don't want to, maybe you could—

PATSY. *(Hatches a plan. Sly.)* On second thought, maybe I *should* pitch in, just to show there's no hard feelings…especially since everyone in Fayro will be there.

SLOGGETT. That's the spirit! Heck, we can all work together and get this thing done. *(Unnoticed, Joveeta storms in hall doorway with a croquet mallet, springs up on the desk chair.)* Because we're all filled with holiday love and joy and— *(Joveeta slams the mallet on the desk several times.)*

JOVEETA. *(Wild-eyed.)* Who's got the big gavel *now*, huh? *(The others freeze. She wields the mallet.)* We are here for a town meeting, and a meeting *will be had*!

BIG ETHEL. *(Contrite.)* Take it away, Your Honor. *(Puts her gavel on the desk.)*

CAPRICE. You know, if you had a man, you'd probably be less tense.

JOVEETA. *(Snaps.)* I wouldn't cross a mayor with a mallet, Mama! *(Steps off chair.)* Now back to business. We've got a big problem. We've worked our butts off starting this new town, but for some reason, the County Commissioners haven't sent us our final papers. I've tried to reach *every single one of them*, but no one returns my calls. It's like they're avoiding me.

GEORGIA DEAN. Maybe they're afraid. *(Gently takes the mallet.)*

I know I am.

JOVEETA. Until we have those papers signed, sealed and delivered, we're not legitimate. In the meantime, it'll only help show how committed we are to our success as an independent town by coming up with ways to increase our revenues.

BABY. I've got one! I been workin' on this since you told me about it last night. I know what will bring people to Doublewide to spend their money…and this is big. *(He's on fire.)* An outlet mall! I mean, they got 'em everywhere, why not here? In fact, I've already made a deal for our first store—Cousin Belita's End Of Time Survival Depot.

JOVEETA. Selling what?

BABY. Whatever hasn't sold at the Survival Depot H.Q. over in Sweetgum. Belita thought for sure there'd be mushroom clouds by Thanksgivin' and she overstocked panic room chem toilets. She's also throwin' in newly expired food items and I figure we'll sell 'em out of the tool shed.

CAPRICE. Is that genius or what? I told Baby his idea is a winner. *(Pulls a bag from behind the sofa.)* And since folks love rubbing elbows with a celebrity, I've decided to indulge my fans. I'm openin' a boutique selling Caprice Crumpler memorabilia. *(Takes out a coat, negligee and a hand mixer missing one beater.)*

JOVEETA. That's just the old junk you couldn't unload at our last yard sale. And didn't I give you that coat for your birthday?

CAPRICE. *(Quickly stuffs the items into the bag.)* The *point*, Joveeta, is that *some* of us are working to increase the revenue stream into Doublewide.

LARK. Ooh! I can set up a "food court" outside the tool shed and sell my Yammy Doublewide Health Bars. Get it? I make them extra wide and cover them with whipped tofu sweetened with agave syrup. In fact, I made a batch for tonight. *(Nauseated, the others try to make sounds of approval as Lark exits into kitchen.)*

PATSY. Would someone just knock me in the head with that mallet? *(Caprice grabs the mallet from Georgia Dean, heads toward Patsy, Baby stops her.)*

GEORGIA DEAN. You know, this *small mall* idea might really catch on.

BIG ETHEL. *(Pulls Caprice's negligee out of bag.)* I'll bet even those Presbyterians in Sweetgum would sneak over here for racy stuff like this. *(To Caprice.)* Just don't let anyone at Stairway to Heaven know you're hawkin' this kind of thing. My hands are *full* keepin' those geezers calmed down.

JOVEETA. Hmm. I'm not convinced this is our answer. I mean, isn't there something more impressive that would get Texans to come all the way to Doublewide and spend good money? *(Lark exits kitchen with a tray of bars.)*

LARK. Don't these smell yummy and yammy? And I found the funniest thing in that crate, Georgia Dean. *(Pulls a yam out of her pocket, hands it to her.)* That looks like a face, doesn't it?

GEORGIA DEAN. *(Snaps to attention.)* Good lord! It does! And it's…it's…

BIG ETHEL. You're white as a sheet. Give me that thing before you go into shock and— *(Grabs the yam, studies it.)* Sweet heavenly days! It's— *(The others all crowd around.)*

SLOGGETT. *(He gasps.)* It's *her!*

LARK. Who?! Is she a saint or something?

CAPRICE. Dang straight! This yam is the spittin' image of—

BABY. *(Cradles the yam in his hands.)* Lady-Bird-Johnson!

ALL. *(Reverent.)* Wow!

BIG ETHEL. Talk about a Christmas miracle!

JOVEETA. Well, we could be on to something. Texans are fool enough to drive *miles* to see something like this. I think Mrs. LBJ might've just saved our bacon!

GEORGIA DEAN. A mall *and* a roadside attraction? Y'all, this is wonderful! Hey, I've got a couple of six-packs and a pot of pintos at my place. Let's go celebrate!

BABY. Beer and beans?! *Par-tay!! (They all rush to front door, open it. SFX: Loud, angry chattering raccoons! He slams the door.)* I forgot. The porch is swarmin' with ticked-off raccoons. We're trapped!

SLOGGETT. We've got to find a way to distract those animals so we can escape. One of us will have to sacrifice ourself to save the rest.

CAPRICE. *(Takes a slug of beer.)* Well, this is obviously a job for a woman and I know exactly who it has to be. *(Opens door, calls outside.)* Fresh meat comin' in! *(In a flash, without warning, grabs Patsy, shoves her out the door. Slams the door. SFX: Animals screech! Patsy screams. Then, to the others.)* Whee! Is it just me or is it beginnin' to feel a lot like Christmas? *(Blackout.)*

Scene 6

Afternoon. Five days later, two days before Christmas Eve. Joveeta, in trousers, shirt and accessories, struggles to balance, perched on a large exercise ball, talks on her phone.

JOVEETA. ...No, no! Please don't put me on hold again. Please! I can't take any more of that music. I— *(Holds phone away from her ear, groans.)* Ahhh!!! I really, really *don't* want a hippopotamus for Christmas! I— *(Then, into phone.)* Hello? Hello?... I have *called* many times! Six times this week, in fact... *(Caprice, in satin pajamas, a short robe trimmed in marabou, matching slippers, flashy earrings, enters front door, eavesdrops.)* As mayor of Doublewide, I have the right to talk with the County Commissioners. It's *very* important that I—

CAPRICE. *(Grabs the phone.)* Listen up, pencil pusher! We pay your salary so stop checking your personal email, get your head out of your butt and *do your job!* Get one of those know-nothin' Commissioners to call us *now* or we will be all over you like ugly on an armadillo! And F.Y.I., we know where you live. *(Hangs up.)*

JOVEETA. Mama, you can't talk to the Commissioner's office like that!

CAPRICE. Sure I can. That's how a Texas woman *gets it done.* You're welcome.

JOVEETA. The last thing I want to do is antagonize the Commissioners. Their silence makes me *very* suspicious. *(Winces, rubs her back.)*

CAPRICE. *(Re: ball.)* I'm not one to mess in anyone's business, but that's the dumbest chair I've ever seen.

JOVEETA. You're the *first person* to mess in *everyone's* business and this isn't a chair, it's an exercise ball. *(Stands, stretches.)* My back's trying to blow out with the stress from town business, the manger competition and the new outlet mall.

CAPRICE. And we've got lots of customers out there. Caprice's Celebrity Corner is a hit. But the store that's getting the most action is the Survival Depot Outlet. Although I suspect some of those *shoppers* may just be gawkers.

JOVEETA. What would they be gawking at? *(Baby bursts through front door dressed like an elf—hat, short pants, tunic top all made of camouflage fabric.)*

BABY. Woo! I am officially sold out of slightly expired flares! Man, it's goin' great, except I ticked off the raccoons again. I moved their stove to make room for more parkin' and I know they're plottin' revenge.

JOVEETA. What on earth are you wearing?

BABY. Not what I wanted, but it's all I could come up with. Y'all know I've *always* dreamed of playin' Santa, but Belita says she gets first dibs on wearin' the Santa suit at Survival H.Q. Just breaks my heart. *(Sees ball.)* Ooh, new chair! Perfect for watchin' *Dancin' with the Stars!* *(Sits on it, wipes out.)* Or not.

CAPRICE. Speaking of *stars*, we all know Cee Cee Windham's *Hospitality House* is the most popular cable access show in the tri-county area. She runs my commercials for Womble's Funeral Home and they're super popular. So I'm gonna tell her I'd be willing to come do a spot for our mall. Want to see what I've come up with?

JOVEETA. No! Not now. Not ever.

CAPRICE. Well, thank you Ms. Killjoy. That's what I get for bein' a team player.

JOVEETA. If I survive this Christmas, it'll be a miracle. I need aspirin—but I'd settle for proof I was swapped at birth. *(A hand on her back, one her head, exits hall doorway. Georgia Dean races in front door.)*

GEORGIA DEAN. Baby, those raccoons are in your shed making off with your dehydrated green bean casseroles.

BABY. No! They're my best sellers! I *knew* they were up to somethin'! *(Exits front door.)*

CAPRICE. Holy cow, what's wrong with you? You look like four flat tires.

GEORGIA DEAN. I'm whupped! I've gone out every night trying to wring as much as I can out of that dating club membership. And I have learned a *very* important lesson from this week-long freak fest I've just endured. When men my age are *single*, odds are there's a *real* good reason.

CAPRICE. Girl, I know you. You're still comparing every man you meet to Nash Sloggett. You gotta lower your standards. At our age, it's slim pickin's in the dating patch. *(Sloggett enters hall doorway, is taken aback by Caprice's presence.)* Speaking of slim pickin's, hey, old timer. Can I bring you a cool one?

SLOGGETT. No thanks, I'm good. *(She exits into kitchen. He crosses to Georgia Dean. Anxious, low.)* I'm *not* good! I've *got* to talk to someone. I haven't slept in three nights! I keeping having these, uh... *(Embarrassed.) suggestive* dreams...

GEORGIA DEAN. Well, that's alright. It's allowed. You're a healthy man.

SLOGGETT. They're about *Caprice!* Ever since I saw her naked, *it's all I see! (Grabs her.)* Swear you won't tell her! *(Caprice exits kitchen with a beer.)*

CAPRICE. Well, I better get back to my fans 'cause they— *(Spots something on the floor.)* Hey, candy cane! *(Turns around, bends over, picks up the candy, unconsciously aims her behind at Sloggett, wiggles it excitedly. He gasps, clutches Georgia Dean. Unaware, Caprice stands. Re: candy cane.)* You don't get your hands on something this delicious every day. Well, back to work. *(Exits front door.)*

SLOGGETT. *(Croaks.)* Water! Gotta have water! *(Races into kitchen as Joveeta enters hall doorway, walks slowly, moans, clearly in pain.)*

GEORGIA DEAN. Girlfriend, that does not sound good. *(Helps her to the ball.)*

JOVEETA. It's my fault, I took on way too much. I promised everyone I could make this town a reality and I owe it to y'all to get Doublewide up and going. And if my back's broke and I can't walk when it's over, so be it. I cannot fail at this!

GEORGIA DEAN. Now, stop that! *(Drapes Joveeta face down over the ball.)* We know you've worked yourself to the bone trying to make this dream come true. You have to know we all look up to you. *(Stops, studies Joveeta slumped helplessly over the ball.)* Okay, maybe not so much this very minute, but *normally. (Lark with Arden Rose in the snuggly and Patsy in coveralls, pearls and dress flats enter front door.)*

LARK. Hey, you two have got to come out and see the crowd. Everyone's buying my yam cookies and shopping. And you were so right, those Texans have *lined up* to see Mrs. Johnson on a sweet potato. It's so exciting…and weird!

JOVEETA. And that's saying a lot coming from a native of *Oregon!*

PATSY. Baby says there's more electrical tape under the sink. I'll just go grab it.

GEORGIA DEAN. You've really thrown yourself into this manger competition. With two days left before Christmas Eve, we couldn't pull this off without you.

PATSY. Since the entire county's going to be there for the judging, a lot's on the line. I intend to give them an entry that will *rock their world! (Exits into kitchen.)*

GEORGIA DEAN. Here, Lark. Arden Rose has worked hard enough selling cookies today. I'll put her down for her nap. *(Whispers to the baby as she exits hall doorway.)* Geor-gia-Dean, Geor-gia-Dean. *(Caprice pokes her head in front door.)*

CAPRICE. I got big news! A fella's out here who works for Totally Texas Television, says they'd like to come back with a crew and do a piece on Doublewide, how we're trying to get our new town up on its feet. Being the local celebrity who knows how to handle herself on TV, I graciously accepted his offer.

JOVEETA. Mama, *I'm* the Mayor of Doublewide, *I* make the decisions. We don't know those TV people. While our status with the County is still pending, we can't run the risk of it being negative publicity. I'll go tell him we can't do it.

CAPRICE. *(Deflated.)* I'll say this for you, you're consistent, *Ms. Dream Crusher.* But if you're the Mayor, you can't go limping out there like the town drunk. Let me do it. I'll let him down easy…like I do all my men. *(Exits front door.)*

LARK. Well, what's cool is that a television program *knows* about us. *(Patsy enters from kitchen with tape.)* But all in all, it's shaping up to be a wonderful first Christmas for Arden Rose. I think it's because we're all together. *(Low.)* I just wish I was having better luck finding my dad and getting him here. That would make this Christmas perfect for Grandpa, too. *(Georgia Dean enters hall doorway.)*

PATSY. Speaking of perfect, I have to give y'all credit on that yam idea. There are hordes of people out there. When it comes to going overboard and making a fool of themselves, no one tops a Texan. *(Big Ethel bursts through front door dressed like Lyndon Johnson— man's suit, string tie, Stetson, cowboy boots.)*

BIG ETHEL. *(À la LBJ.)* My fellow Americans, we need to talk.

GEORGIA DEAN. I thought O.C. was dressing up like Lyndon Johnson.

BIG ETHEL. He *was* until we discovered he'd packed on so many pounds since Thanksgivin' he couldn't squeeze into the suit pants. But I'm glad to do it 'cause that tater's makin' us money hand over fist. But that's not what I'm here to talk about, we got us a situation— *(Baby yanks open front door.)*

BABY. We got us a situation! There's a weird-lookin' gal in a hat and sunglasses waitin' to see Lady Bird. I swear it's Loydene Buttram, the cow inseminator from Fayro in disguise and she's real nervous. Think she's here to shoplift or somethin'?

JOVEETA. *(Painfully gets to her feet.)* Nope. I know *exactly* what she's doing.

BIG ETHEL. *(To Baby.)* And F.Y.I., Loydene retired from inseminatin' after she got the carpal tunnel.

JOVEETA. That's right and then she got herself on the County Commissioners' Board and has kept her nose in everybody's business ever since. *(Anger grows.)* She's obviously in disguise because she couldn't resist coming to see Lady Bird but she doesn't want *me* to know she's here. *But I know now. (Starts for front door.)*

GEORGIA DEAN. Where do you think you're going?

JOVEETA. To make Loydene Buttram squeal. That ex-inseminator *will* tell me, once and for all, why the County Commissioners are avoiding me. Come on, Baby, you're my backup. *(Limps out front door, Baby on her heels.)*

BIG ETHEL. *(Calls out the door.)* Just don't make a scene!

LARK. She won't! Joveeta's the mayor, a professional. She knows how to conduct herself like an adult. *(Beat. They stare at each other.)*

PATSY. Five bucks says she makes a scene. *(Slaps a five-dollar bill on the desk.)*

BIG ETHEL. I say it's a *big* one. *(Quickly pulls out a bill, slaps it on the desk.)*

GEORGIA DEAN. And I say it's *so* big an intervention will be required. *(Pulls a bill from her pocket, slaps it on the desk. Sloggett enters from kitchen, looks around.)*

SLOGGETT. *(Anxious.)* Is it safe? Is Caprice gone? What's going on?

LARK. We've got a situation outside, but Joveeta's on it. *(To Big Ethel.)* Sorry Baby stole your thunder about the big story.

BIG ETHEL. Actually, that's a whole *different* situation than what I came in to talk about. We've got us an emergency. My cousin Geneva over in Fayro called and she just found out that sanctimonious LaMerle Minshew lied about Sweetgum's entry in the competition, hopin' to surprise everyone. Their theme is *exactly* the same as ours. *(Everyone gasps.)*

SLOGGETT. They're doing *Nativity At The North Pole*, too?

BIG ETHEL. Bingo! They've had weeks to work on it and have poured beaucoup bucks into their display. *(Everyone groans.)* I hear the Verdeen gals even rented penguin costumes. They're gonna be in the igloo with the Holy Family!

GEORGIA DEAN. *We* should've thought of that. How can we compete with that kind of brilliance? We can't show up with some lame second-best entry.

LARK. Poor Baby! He was so looking forward to his dream coming true by playing Santa at our Manger. He even bought Legos as his gift for the newborn King.

BIG ETHEL. So this means we've only got *two days* to come up with a new theme and build it!

SLOGGETT. That's not enough time. Maybe we should pull out.

PATSY. No! No way! We've got to be in that competition. I've got too much riding on it! They can't do this to me! *(Off their surprised looks.)* I mean…to my…daughter-in-law, Tina Jo. Because…it'll break her heart if we up and quit. *(Intensity grows.)* So, I'll tell you exactly what we're going to do. We'll come up with an idea, work twenty-four-seven and *get it built.* We *will* participate in this Nativity Smackdown…or die trying! *(Races out hall doorway.)*

SLOGGETT. Wow. That sister of mine sure is full of the holiday spirit.

BIG ETHEL. *(Low to Georgia Dean.)* She's full of something alright. *(To the others.)* But she *is* right about one thing, we can make this happen. We're gonna do somethin' great and do it with our usual class and dignity. *(Baby opens front door. He and Caprice help Joveeta limp in. Clothes torn, Joveeta holds a woman's wig.)*

CAPRICE. Joveeta ripped into Loydene Buttram like a wildcat. You can't believe the scene they made. That jug-eared preacher from Tinsel had to break it up.

GEORGIA DEAN. Told you so! I win the bet! *(Scoops up the cash.)*

BABY. Joveeta *did* try talkin' to Loydene first. But when she turned tail and took off runnin', Joveeta had no choice but to tackle her. I was real proud.

JOVEETA. Okay, maybe I lost my cool, but at least I finally got *one* of the Commissioners to talk to me—admittedly it was while I had her pinned to the ground, but still. Loydene started blathering about how an "unsustainable" trailer park like Doublewide that decides to be a town will only drain county resources and will never be approved. See? They're trying to crush us so we don't inspire other people to break away from bigger towns and threaten their tax bases. It's all about the money…as usual.

SLOGGETT. God forbid us little people get a say in our own destiny. They must still be ticked that we tried to secede from Texas. But hell, everybody does that.

JOVEETA. *(Rubs her back.)* Here's the real kicker. The Commissioners found an obscure hundred-year-old law that says a town isn't recognized as such unless it shows population growth. Loydene says if we want that approval, we have to prove our population has doubled *by the end of the year*!

LARK. But…that's next week! We'd have to get ten more people to move here by New Year's!

JOVEETA. You got it. If we don't, they won't validate our incorporation.

GEORGIA DEAN. So, Doublewide is being double-crossed! I'm getting it now. That way, they undo everything we worked so hard for and Tugaloo will finally be able to annex this property after all.

CAPRICE. This might sound odd coming from someone who sleeps in caskets for a living, but we are *not* gonna take this lying down!

SLOGGETT. You said it! Texas had to fight for independence more than once and if *we* have to fight for our independence again, so be it. *(Excited, the others cheer.)*

BIG ETHEL. We're not going to let the big guys roll over us like this. We're gonna fight 'em and we're gonna win! *(The others cheer.)*

BABY. Doublewide forever! Power to the people! *(The others cheer loudly.)*

LARK. We'll have a sit-in at the Courthouse, burn some sage and follow it up with a peace meditation! *(She cheers…alone.)*

GEORGIA DEAN. Hon, time to leave *Oregon* behind. Embrace your *inner Texan*.

LARK. Oh, okay. *(Summons her dark side.)* We'll crush those shidepokes under our boot heels until they cry for mercy, but *there won't be any*! *(The others cheer.)*

JOVEETA. Alright! We just have to find ten people who'll move to Doublewide by the end of next week. We can do this! *(Cheers.)* They think they've beaten us, but they're about to see some *fight*!

BABY. That's right! We need all the firepower we can get! Let's turn them raccoons loose on 'em!

JOVEETA. Okay, let's get a plan. Mama, what I said about your commercial, I take it all back. You get yourself on *Hospitality House*, but don't be hawking your *celebrity leavin's*. You're going to hard sell the good life in Doublewide.

CAPRICE. And I am just the celebrity who can do it.

BIG ETHEL. Well, LBJ's hittin' the trail again, but this time it's not for votes, I'm stumpin' for new residents for Doublewide. *(Storms out front door.)*

SLOGGETT. I'll get on the blower and call my old Army buddies. They're retirees and I bet they'd love to live out here in all this peace and quiet.

CAPRICE. Start dialing, Sarge! Make sure there's some cute widowers in the bunch! *(Slaps his butt. Sloggett, rattled, exits front door.)* Baby! Lark! We've got payin' customers out there. Let's keep this mall rockin'. *(Exits front door.)*

LARK. *(Calls.)* I'll check on Arden Rose. Be right there! *(Exits hall doorway.)*

JOVEETA. Baby, there may be potential residents out there, so work the crowd! *(Staggers over to the ball, collapses on it face down.)*

BABY. I'm on it. You just take care of that back, Joveeta. We need all the spine you got. *(Pumped up.)* There's nothin' we can't do! We're Texans! And nothin's gonna stop— *(Opens front door, the raccoon flies in, attacks him. Baby screams, tries to fight it off as he staggers out front door, out of view.)*

GEORGIA DEAN. *(Calls.)* Bandit, don't kill Baby! We need him for our population count! *(Races out front door. Joveeta is still slumped over the ball as lights dim. Instrumental Texas swing Christmas music comes up softly as far downstage right a spotlight comes up on Lark and Arden Rose.)*

LARK. Oh, Arden Rose, who knew living in Texas would be so exciting? And I'm doing all I can to find my daddy and get him home. Grandpa Sloggett will be so happy. It will be a Christmas we'll never forget! *(Spotlight goes out. Spotlight comes up far downstage left on Patsy, who holds a drill.)*

PATSY. *(Sinister, to herself.)* If I have to do this by myself, I will. Nothing's going to stop me. They'll pay for what they did. I am going to make this a Christmas they'll never forget. *(Cackles diabolically, revs drill as spotlight goes out. Lights come up on the trailer. Joveeta raises her head heavenward.)*

JOVEETA. Okay, if you've been watching what's going on down here, I'm begging you, something's *got* to work out for us. We've come so far, we just can't fail now. These good people are doing their best. If you could just give us this one break, it'll be a Christmas we'll never forget— *(Just then, Baby races in far downstage right, screams, runs straight across stage, a raccoon attached to his head, another attached to his leg, exits far downstage left. Beat. She sighs, shakes her head.)* —no matter how hard we try. *(Music comes up full. Blackout.)*

End of Act One

ACT TWO

Scene 1

Christmas Eve morning. A spotlight comes up downstage center on Big Ethel in scrubs and reindeer antlers. She carries a flashlight, addresses the audience.

BIG ETHEL. Alright, folks, let's settle down. I know today is Christmas Eve, we just need to go over a few things. On behalf of management here at Stairway to Heaven, I need to remind y'all we're leavin' outta here at five o'clock this afternoon, so get to the van early and get you a seat so we can leave on time. It's gonna be a spectacular evenin'. Every town in the county's competin' at the Tabernacle's Battle of the Mangers with their unique and innovative tributes to that world-changin' event in Bethlehem. *(Reads from a list.)* Sweetgum's entry is called "North Pole Nativity," Fayro's takin' us to Hawaii with their "Poi To The World," Tugaloo's got 'em a *Star Wars* theme—"A Long Time Ago In A Galaxy Far, Far Away In A Manger," Hmm. That's right cute. The little town of Tinsel's puttin' a twist on "We Three Kings"—*their* kings bein' Martin Luther, Billie Jean and Carole. Finally—and y'all are the *first* to know—I'm proud to announce our new town of Doublewide is in it to win it with a pure-T for Texas entry, "Nativity At The Alamo"! Yes-sir-ee, we've got us a line-up of Lone Star heroes backin' up Little Baby J—with William Travis, Jim Bowie and the one and only *(Pats her heart.)* Davy Crockett. Let's see 'em top that! So y'all enjoy yourselves. Now, let me wrap this up right quick by introducin' Lark Barken, whom you may know from Bronco Betty's Buffeteria. Come on in, Lark. *(Lark waves at everyone as she enters from the back of the house and hurries to the front rows. She wears slacks, a Christmas sweater, a Santa hat, carries a handful of flyers. Arden Rose is in her snuggly also in a Santa hat.)* Now start passin' out them flyers, Lark, and spread 'em around, we don't have a lot. *(Lark does so.)* See, folks, we're in the business of increasin' Doublewide's population A.S.A.P., and we're callin' this campaign *Doublin' Doublewide*. We know all of *you* are here 'til the roll is called up yonder, but this is your golden opportunity to get your family to move closer to you. Now I realize that notion doesn't appeal to *everyone* here, but haven't the rest of you occasionally been struck by the thought: What the devil are my kids up to now? Be honest, how many of you don't trust your family as far as you can throw 'em? Show of hands? *(Strafes the audience with the flashlight.)*

LARK. *(Waves to Ethel, calls.)* Here's one, Big Ethel! *(Pulls an audience member to his feet.)* This nice man here doesn't really trust his family at all!

BIG ETHEL. *(Shines flashlight on him.)* Matter of fact, I know some of your people and you are so right to have concerns. And thanks for sharin'. Let's give him a round of applause. *(Claps.)* I'm sure there are more of you out there with trust issues, so take one of these flyers, it's got all the information you'll need for your family to move immediately to Doublewide. And when I say "immediately," I mean by next Tuesday. So get on it, people. *We* need your family to live in our town and *you* need your family close by to make sure they're not goin' through your money like Sherman burnin' through Georgia! So Merry Christmas, everyone. Remember to get your family jazzed about movin' to Doublewide, remember to get on the van by five and most of all, *Remember The Alamo*! *(Blackout.)*

Scene 2

Later that day. Lights come up on Joveeta's living room. The dinette table is set with plates, silverware, glasses for two. A small, sparsely decorated Christmas tree sits on the desk, mistletoe hangs above front door. Sloggett enters front door.

SLOGGETT. *(Calls.)* Baby Crumpler, it is done! Our mall's officially closed for Christmas! *(Caprice enters from hall doorway in a long bathrobe.)*

CAPRICE. Yeah, and we did right good, too.

SLOGGETT. *(Startled.)* Caprice! You still here? I figured you'd be over in Sweetgum doing that commercial by now.

CAPRICE. I'm about to leave but I wanted to talk to you first. I've noticed you're looking bad lately. I mean, even worse than usual. What's up with that?

SLOGGETT. *(Covers.)* Uh…a little insomnia. No big deal.

CAPRICE. Well, I've got just the thing to give you some sweet dreams. *(Her back to the audience, she opens her bathrobe, appears to flash Sloggett, does a little shimmy. Sloggett screams, backs away, covers his face. She laughs, drops the robe, she's fully dressed in sparkly, glittery leggings, sexy sweater.)* Had you going there, didn't I? *(Sexy.)* Do you see me looking like this once you're all tucked in?

SLOGGETT. *(Ticked.)* Dang it! Georgia Dean told you! She swore she wouldn't.

CAPRICE. Get real. Women always tell each other stuff like that. It's how we keep running the world behind your backs. *(Grabs the robe.)* Well, I'm off to save our town and delight my fans with a dazzling display of *me!* See you in dreamland, *hot stuff. (Laughs, exits front door.)*

SLOGGETT. *(Calls after her.)* I am never closing my eyes again, *ever!* (Baby exits the kitchen wearing a frilly apron, oven mitt on each hand, carries a casserole dish. Sloggett averts his eyes.) Oh, good lord, I spoke too soon!

BABY. I just made us a bite to eat since we'll be busy settin' up and bein' in our Alamo nativity and won't have time for supper. *(Removes mitts, serves the plates.)*

SLOGGETT. Oh. That's real thoughtful, nice surprise.

BABY. Speakin' of surprises, any luck finding your son?

SLOGGETT. Not a lick. I've tried everything I can think of but looks like he doesn't want to be found and I can only blame myself. I broke up Nash and Georgia Dean when they were just love-struck kids and then my mule-headedness drove him away. I'd give anything to take it all back now.

BABY. I know what you mean about regret—I wish I hadn't ever crossed those raccoons. I had a bunch of out-of-date fireworks I was countin' on sellin' for New Year's. Folks would've really gone for 'em and I could've gotten a good price, too. But when my back was turned I know those raccoons took 'em. Out of pure spite. *(They sit, eat.)*

SLOGGETT. You've really gone above and beyond whipping up this casserole.

BABY. Well, we're all goin' above and beyond this Christmas. Like for the competition, Mr. O.C. collected all them milk jugs for the igloo, and when we switched themes, Patsy stayed up all night paintin' those jugs to look like adobe bricks for the Alamo.

SLOGGETT. Yeah, I'm proud of her. Weren't we lucky Patsy's roommate at the insane asylum kept her keys to the County Museum and let us borrow those costumes?

BABY. Personally, I think we've got a real shot at winnin'. And Patsy told me she's got a big treat up her sleeve for the presentation to the judges.

SLOGGETT. Well, I think this *casserole's* a big treat. I like the marshmallow topping…and do I taste cinnamon in this?

BABY. It's my secret weapon. I made us a big batch 'cause Lark told us not to let the rest of those yams go to waste—but there's still half a bushel left. *(Takes another bite.)*

SLOGGETT. That's good, long as you didn't use the one in the draining rack. So many people had handled it, Lark said she felt it was only right to give Lady Bird a good face washing. *(Takes a bite. Baby, horrified, jumps to his feet.)*

BABY. *(Screams.)* Oh my God… I did! I didn't know! I put that one in the casserole! I chunked up Lady Bird! We're eatin' her now! *(Sloggett jumps to his feet.)* Oh, no! Joveeta's gonna kill me! *(Races into the kitchen.)*

SLOGGETT. Baby, noooo! The Bird was our meal ticket and now…she *is our meal! (Plunges his hands into the casserole, pulls out a glob of yams, desperately tries to shape a face.)* Maybe we can put her back together! *(Baby races out of the kitchen with a basket of yams, plops basket on the sofa downstage center.)*

BABY. *(Shouts.)* Forget it! She's gone! We gotta find another face! *(Yanks out yam after yam.)*

SLOGGETT. Look for Lincoln! Reba! Tom Brady! Anybody! *(Baby digs furiously, they look at one another, scream. Blackout.)*

Scene 3

Later that day. A spotlight comes up downstage left on Caprice in the "cable access studio" beside a Hospitality House *sign that's framed with tinsel. Caprice faces the audience as she talks with the unseen stage technician, Harley. He responds to her via a microphone.*

CAPRICE. *(Shades her eyes.)* Harley, I tell you every time, these lights are too dang bright, they're gonna show every wrinkle I've got. Can't you give me something soft and flatterin' that'll make me look better?

HARLEY. *(Voiceover.)* You bet. How about I throw a wool blanket over your head?

CAPRICE. Don't be giving me any lip, Harley Dobbs. You best do your job and make me look gorgeous in this commercial. My fans expect it.

HARLEY. *(Voiceover.)* I bet they do...both of 'em. Let's roll in five, four, three, two—

CAPRICE. *(Faces audience, addresses "the camera.")* Howdy, fellow Texans! Caprice Crumpler here and I want to talk to you about the true meaning of Christmas. Some say it's "joy and love." But I say that's a bunch of hooey. Christmas is about a *new start* and I bet lots of y'all are searching for just that. So what better way to start fresh than to leave the dead weight of your old life behind? I'm talking pulling up stakes and relocating. Yes, indeed! Ditch that albatross of a mortgage from around your neck and move to the brand-new bustling municipality of Doublewide. That big house? Give it up! All that yard work? Give it up! All that stress? Give it up! Yes, *give up* and move to Doublewide. I'm talking freedom, y'all. Our motto is live and let live and what better time to reinforce that than Christmas? And to that end, I feel a song coming on! *(Sings a lively ditty,*

to the tune of "O Little Town of Bethlehem.")
> O LITTLE TOWN OF DOUBLEWIDE
> THE SWEETEST IN THE STATE
> COME CHANGE YOUR LIFE
> GIVE UP YOUR STRIFE
> BEFORE IT'S ALL TOO LATE
> ENJOY A DOSE OF FREEDOM
> WITH A CELEBRITY
> YOU'RE IN A RUT?
> GET OFF YOUR BUTT
> AND MOVE IN NEXT TO ME.

(Waves at the camera.) See y'all in Doublewide! *(Beat.)*

HARLEY. *(Voiceover.)* And…cut. You *are* done, right? Please God tell me you're done.

CAPRICE. That went great! We'll have to fight off all the new residents once this ad starts running. What do you think?

HARLEY. *(Voiceover.)* I think they don't pay me *nearly* enough to do this job. *(Blackout.)*

Scene 4

Later that day. Lights come up on Joveeta's living room. Georgia Dean, in a Christmas sweater and slacks, places dishes and utensils into a pan. Joveeta limps in hall doorway in a form-fitting blouse, pair of slacks. She rubs her back.

JOVEETA. Arden Rose is fine. I just checked to make sure she's still asleep.

GEORGIA. Don't tell lies on Christmas Eve, woman! You were in there whispering your name to that baby so it would be the first word she says.

JOVEETA. How do you know that?

GEORGIA DEAN. Because *I* went in there to whisper *my* name and you were hogging all the space at the crib. *(Scrubs a spot on the floor.)*

40

JOVEETA. What *are* you doing?

GEORGIA DEAN. Cleaning up a big mess of sweet potatoes. Did you have a food fight in here or something? *(Lark enters from kitchen.)*

LARK. Speaking of that, this morning I washed Lady Bird off and left her on the sink to dry but her looks have…changed. Now she looks more like…Shrek.

GEORGIA DEAN. Well, no woman looks her best right after a facial.

JOVEETA. So what's *your* excuse? You look positively whupped today.

GEORGIA DEAN. It's a miracle I can even sit up and take nourishment after last night. Worst date in the history of womankind! The jerk was late, hadn't bothered to put on a clean shirt and the first thing he said to me was, "You didn't sound this fat on the phone." And it went *downhill* from there. That's it! I am *done* with men. I'm embracing my spinsterhood. From here on, I'm wearing granny panties, growing leg hair and adopting a herd of cats.

JOVEETA. You already *have* a herd of cats *and* raccoons *and* squirrels. So if you ever *do* consider dating again, what you *should* embrace is a veterinarian. *(Glances down the hall. To others, low.)* Okay, it's time to talk. We're alone, right?

GEORGIA DEAN. *(Dramatic.)* Yes, we are. All alone in a lonely world.

JOVEETA. Shake it off, drama queen. I'm talking about our schedule tonight.

LARK. Well, I think everything's ready, but honestly, I feel really guilty that we haven't told the others what we're doing.

JOVEETA. This is for the greater good. Luckily when I re-contacted the guy from Totally Texas Television, they were still excited about doing a piece on Doublewide. But I only agreed we'd be part of it if it was *live*.

GEORGIA DEAN. That is so smart, Madam Mayor. This way they can't edit it and make us look bad.

JOVEETA. We only get five minutes to make our case and sell folks on our town. That's why I *had* to throw everyone else off the scent, especially Mama, so we can do a *dignified* presentation that makes people want to move to Doublewide.

GEORGIA DEAN. I'm just sorry we have to miss the manger

competition to do it. But remember, Lark, we're telling everyone we'll be there to cheer them on.

LARK. *You* tell them. I can't lie. I even think about lying, I get terribly nauseous.

JOVEETA. You're going to be fine. And we need you and Arden Rose on camera so folks will know Doublewide's multigenerational and family friendly.

GEORGIA DEAN. She's right. Shoot, we bag us one Mormon couple with eight kids and we're done!

JOVEETA. Truth is, everything's on the line for Doublewide tonight, so we all just need to stay calm. I mean, look at me—cool as a cucumber—nothing to be nervous about. *(Patsy sticks her head in front door.)*

PATSY. *(Barks.)* Hey! *(All three girls jump and scream. Oblivious, she storms in like General Patton.)* Okay, we're two hours away from the Nativity Smackdown and we are ready to launch. The Alamo's on the flatbed, I've got the baby doll for the manger, costumes, everything I need except a hat for Jim Bowie.

JOVEETA. I've got that!

PATSY. Well, don't just stand there admiring my efforts. Go, go, go! Get it now! *(Startled, Joveeta rubs her back as she quickly limps out hall doorway.)*

GEORGIA DEAN. Wow, Patsy! You really *did* save our bacon coming up with the Alamo idea at the last minute. You've done a remarkable job.

PATSY. Where there's a woman, there's a way. *(To Lark.)* And you're all going to be there. *(Lark puts her hand on her stomach.)* Right? *(Lark covers her mouth, races into the kitchen.)* What's the matter with her?

GEORGIA DEAN. I bet she's O.D.'d on those Yammy Tofu Health Bars. Too much of a good thing is still too much. *(Joveeta enters hall doorway with a hat.)*

JOVEETA. This should fit Big Ethel, I mean *Jim Bowie*. I sure hope we win, but if we don't, as long as we come in ahead of Tugaloo, I'll be fine with it.

PATSY. Not me. It's all or nothin'. When I'm finished, no one will *ever* forget this competition or the name *Doublewide*. *(Laughs maniacally, exits front door.)*

JOVEETA. You know, Patsy's turned out to be a real team player. Every once in a while, I find myself starting to like her. *(Patsy sticks her head in front door.)*

PATSY. Another thing, Joveeta. You're looking good—and maybe next time they'll have that blouse in your size. *(Exits.)*

JOVEETA. And then I get over it.

GEORGIA DEAN. She has a point. What *are* you wearing for the interview?

JOVEETA. What are you talking about? I'm wearing *this*. What's wrong with it?

GEORGIA DEAN. Besides *everything*? Nothing. Look, we'll run over to my trailer. I picked up a snappy blazer for you over at the church thrift store, Worn Again. *(Disappears behind the sofa to clean.)*

JOVEETA. Fine. I'll wear whatever you got. This whole thing is fairly cobbled together anyway. In fact, since it's Christmas Eve, the television guys didn't have anyone to come over and set up the video and audio feed, so they hired the tech who works on Cee Cee Windham's *Hospitality House*. His name is Harley.

GEORGIA DEAN. *(Pops up from behind sofa, horrified.)* NOOOOO! Not Harley Dobbs! *That's* the jerk I had the horrible date with last night. Rude, conceited, pushy, insulting—a horndog from Mars! You've never met anyone as weird as Harley Dobbs. I told him I never wanted to see him again.

JOVEETA. Well, you're going to see him tonight, so brace yourself.

GEORGIA DEAN. Now *I'm* feeling nauseous. I need energy. I'll go make coffee.

JOVEETA. With so much at stake tonight, girl, we are *way* beyond coffee. *(Gets flask from desk drawer.)* It is half past vodka and a quarter to gin. *(Takes a slug.)*

GEORGIA DEAN. *(Takes flask.)* If this all fails, when we tuck tail and head off into the sunset, I hope someone lifts a glass to us and says, *(As in "'Twas the Night Before Christmas.")* "And I heard them exclaim as they drove toward the west—"

JOVEETA. "Kiss our butts, County Board, 'cause we all did our best!" *(They laugh. Georgia Dean toasts with the flask, knocks one back. Blackout.)*

Scene 5

That night. [This scene takes place in front of the darkened living room set.] A pool of light comes up downstage center "outside Joveeta's trailer." Joveeta, in the same slacks and blouse, stands center stage in front of two tall bushes, faces the audience and listens as Harley, unseen, speaks to her via a microphone.

HARLEY. *(Voiceover.)* Okay, since we're shooting this outdoors, there's only two feet of light on either side of you. If you step out of the light, you're off camera. *(Condescending.)* You *do* see the camera, right?

JOVEETA. A near-sighted orangutan could see it. *(Points to the back of the house, i.e., "the camera.")* I've been looking at it all this time!

HARLEY. *(Voiceover.)* Fine. I have you on the monitor back here in my van so when we're on air live, talk into the camera like you're talking to me now—*but nicer.*

JOVEETA. You can't be that sensitive. This is Doublewide—everybody in town is nice. *(Georgia Dean hustles in stage right, carries a blazer, cosmetic bag.)*

GEORGIA DEAN. *(To camera.)* Drop dead, Harley Dobbs!

HARLEY. *(Voiceover.)* Well, look who's here—Miss-I'd-Rather-French-Kiss-A-Rattlesnake-Than-Go-Out-With-You-Again.

GEORGIA DEAN. *(To camera.)* I said it, I meant it, I stand by it.

JOVEETA. Enough! So you two had a lousy date last night—*move on!* We've got too much at stake for your bickering to get in the way!

GEORGIA DEAN. I'm sorry. You're right. *(Helps Joveeta into blazer.)* We've got bigger fish to catch, so just ignore… *(To Harley.)* the *scum on the pond!*

HARLEY. *(Voiceover.)* So much for peace on earth, good will toward *fine-lookin' men.* Joveeta, I'll ask the questions the Totally Texas TV guys sent and— *(Lark and Arden Rose, in Santa hats, enter stage left. Georgia Dean combs Joveeta's hair.)* Great. *More* females. Just what I need.

LARK. Hey you two, I'm worried. I was listening to Cee Cee Windham on the radio emceeing the manger competition in Fayro and she said hundreds of people showed up. She'd just said how good our Alamo looked when there was a loud bang. Everything went silent. That was ten minutes ago. I hope nothing's wrong.

JOVEETA. I bet it was just a transmission problem. *(Checks her watch.)* But if something *did* cut the festivities short, we've got to hustle. If we don't get this done pronto, our people will be coming home and getting in the way.

HARLEY. *(Voiceover.)* Austin says we're next. There'll be a couple bars of "Jingle Bells," then I say, "This is Totally Texas Television *live* from Doublewide." When you hear that, you're *on*. Start your intro. *(Georgia Dean powders Joveeta's face.)*

JOVEETA. Oh, gosh, I hope my back doesn't blow out. Remember, we have to be convincing enough to get people to move here—*fast*. If we do that, no way the County Board can say we're not a town. They'll *have* to certify us.

GEORGIA DEAN. I'm sure there's enough time for you to do some stretches before you— *(SFX: A few bars of "Jingle Bells." The women clutch each other.)*

HARLEY. *(Voiceover.)* This is Totally Texas Television *live* from Doublewide! *(Georgia Dean scrambles off right out of the light. Joveeta and Lark are now on air.)*

LARK. *(Frozen with fear, stares into "the camera.")* Oh. My. Godddd!

JOVEETA. *(Quickly covers, sings to camera.)* …rest ye merry gentlemen, let nothing you dismay! *(Nervous laugh. Launches into a slightly stilted sales pitch.)* Yes, it *is* Christmas Eve, fellow Texans. I'm Joveeta Crumpler, Mayor of the brand-new town of Doublewide, the sweetest little spot in the Lone Star State. And this is Lark and baby Arden Rose and our Christmas gift to you tonight is to tell you about our wonderful community. Yes, Doublewide offers an easy-going lifestyle in a welcoming multigenerational community, doesn't it, Lark? Lark. *(Smiles, waits as Lark, frozen, stares into camera. Joveeta nudges her.)*

LARK. *(Snaps out of it, speaks rapid-fire.)* Uh…yes. Multigenerational, as you can see here with my daughter, Arden Rose. *(Picks up speed.)* Although you can't see her right now, she's asleep. *(Hiccups.)* But everyone here is kind… *(Hiccups.)* and loving… *(Hiccups twice.)* and attentive to each other. *(Hiccups non-stop.)*

JOVEETA. *(Smiles to camera, gently pushes Lark out of the light. Lark exits stage left.)* Thank you, Lark. Yes, tonight we're inviting folks who dream of living among independent and creative individuals to join us and make *our* home *your* home, too. And we want you to do it *right now.* I mean, *why* put off living a happy life among brand-new old friends?

HARLEY. *(Voiceover.)* So, Mayor Crumpler, what kind of individuals already live here?

JOVEETA. I'm so glad you asked, Interested Texan. *(Now hiccup-free, Lark slides in stage left with three hand-lettered signs. She stands beside Joveeta, stares frozen into the camera, changes the signs as Joveeta speaks to illustrate each point. Lark's first sign reads: "Neighbors you'll want for life.")* Our residents, though small in number, are big-hearted and industrious. *(Lark replaces the sign with another: "A Good Old-Fashioned Community.")* They're kind and mature individuals anyone would love to have living next door. *(Lark's third sign is upside down: "A Big Little Gem In The Heart of Texas." Joveeta quickly turns it right-side up.)* If you're tired of stress and anxiety—and since time is of the essence—get those Christmas gifts opened, then throw the kids in the car and drive to Doublewide and see for yourself what all the excitement's about. *(Sloggett, agitated, dressed as Colonel William Travis, in a Texas Army uniform circa 1830, his face smudged with soot, hurries in stage right.)*

SLOGGETT. I've got to talk to Joveeta! *(Georgia Dean pulls him back, he struggles with her. Lark and Joveeta notice but keep going.)*

JOVEETA. Let your new life start tomorrow. Come on home and experience the tranquility of Doublewide.

SLOGGETT. *(Crosses to Joveeta, drags Georgia Dean along. Sloggett, unaware they're on TV, rants.)* You won't believe what just happened! It was a catastrophe!

JOVEETA. *(Covers, to camera.)* Here's a calm and happy resident of our town now—Haywood Sloggett, one of the founders of our peaceful community.

SLOGGETT. *(Oblivious.)* We'd all gotten into place in front of the Alamo. Jim Bowie, Davy Crockett and I were standing there looking down on the little baby Jesus next to the illuminated Mary and Joseph, the judges were admiring our scene, man alive, we were looking great. Suddenly this blast behind the Alamo knocked us to the ground! Milk jugs were hurtling through the air, it was chaos!

LARK. Please tell me everyone survived the Alamo this time. *(Caprice in a coonskin hat, buckskin fringed shirt and pants, smudged face, races in stage right.)*

CAPRICE. Talk about horrible! It was terrible! I didn't think we'd make it! Sparks were flying, fireworks exploding all around us, but somehow— *(Sees Sloggett, drops the drama.)* How'd *you* get here so fast? You didn't tell it, did you? *I* wanted to. I'm Davy Crockett, the star of the Alamo. It's *my* story!

HARLEY. *(Voiceover. Oblivious.)* So, Mayor Crumpler, what do you have to offer new residents? *(Sloggett and Caprice look around and up for the source of the voice.)*

SLOGGETT. *(Freaked.)* What's that? Who's talking to us?

LARK. *(She, Joveeta and Georgia Dean exchange a look. Covers.)* Uh... God?

GEORGIA DEAN. No, someone who just *thinks* he is. *(Throws a hostile glance at the camera, tries to ease Caprice and Sloggett out stage right.)*

CAPRICE. Wait! I know that voice! I get what's happening here! You're doing that TV interview—without *me*!! *(Georgia Dean moves Sloggett stage right, out of the light.)*

JOVEETA. *(Low.)* Let me just explain—

CAPRICE. Save it, Judas. This is *my* gig. *(Pushes Joveeta away. To camera. She is on!)* Hello, fans. It is I, Caprice Crumpler, we're so happy you're with us tonight. We've got so much for you here in Doublewide. So don't touch that remote, I've got somethin' to tell you as soon as I'm camera-ready. *(Races off stage left.)*

JOVEETA. *(Forges ahead, to camera.)* Yes, it's a colorful group of residents, with *many* stories to tell. And tall tales are what Texas is famous for. In fact—

SLOGGETT. *(Yells after Caprice.)* You don't get to tell every story around here, woman! If I want to tell the next story, *I'll tell it! (Georgia Dean shushes him.)*

JOVEETA. *(To camera.)* We're not some sleepy little country town, this is the place for active living. You can see there's a lot going on here in— *(Raises her arm to gesture, gasps.)* My back! *(Doubles over.)*

LARK. *(Yells.)* I'll go get your ball!

JOVEETA. *(Soldiers through the pain, to camera.)* Because…that's how we are in our town—one for all and all for— *(Falls to her knees in pain.)* one. The residents here are kind and loving friends and neighbors.

HARLEY. *(Voiceover.)* Good to know. *(Pointedly.)* 'Cause there's always a risk that your *older single women* in a town might tend to be uppity, cold-hearted and unbelievably picky. *(Upstage, Sloggett looks around for the source of the voice.)*

GEORGIA DEAN. *(Storms to center stage. To camera, pointedly.)* Which they would never be if the dating pool of available men wasn't contaminated by egotistical, conceited dullards. Happily, the women of Doublewide are intelligent, sophisticated and refined. *(Patsy races in stage left, her face and overalls smudged, her hair fried from fireworks, sticks straight out of her head.)*

PATSY. *(Crows, in ecstasy.)* WOOOOO!! You should've seen it! It was fantastic—fireworks going off in every direction, terrified people running everywhere! And Tina Jo's face—she had no clue what was going on! It was beautiful!

SLOGGETT. *You* did this! *You* stole the fireworks from the Survival Depot Outlet, *you* rigged our entry and *you* almost frightened the town of Fayro to death!

PATSY. *(Unrepentant.)* Yeah, I did it! And it was worth all the work! Tina Jo's big moment was ruined, just like she ruined my life! And nobody's going to make me sorry for any of it! *(Big Ethel dressed as Jim Bowie—fringed buckskin jacket, neckerchief, Western hat—charges onstage with a rifle.)*

BIG ETHEL. Want to bet? *(Patsy whirls around.)* We worked our butts off to gain the respect of the other communities in this county and take our place as a thrivin' legitimate town and you pull this stunt. *And* your fireworks melted our life-size Joseph and Mary into big, old plastic cow patties. If you're not sorry now, you're gonna be! *(Raises her rifle. Patsy screams as Big Ethel chases her off stage right. Lark enters stage left with Joveeta's exercise ball.)*

LARK. I've got the exercise ball— *(Stops, to camera.)* be-cause…here in Doublewide, we believe an athletic, healthy life is a good life. *(Hiccups as she and Georgia Dean maneuver Joveeta, drape her over the ball.)*

GEORGIA DEAN. *(To camera.)* We certainly do. And teamwork is a given in our town. It's a gift Santa won't have to bring us on his rounds tonight.

SLOGGETT. *Santa!* Poor Baby! He finally got his wish to play ol' St. Nick. He squeezed into Belita's Santa Suit and stood up so proud with us at the Alamo. But he was right next to the fireworks when they blew up. Where is he?! *(Joveeta, Georgia Dean and Lark exchange horrified looks. Joveeta struggles, carries on.)*

JOVEETA. *(To camera.)* So, if you want to live in a place where something is always happening, you can't do better than Double-wide. *(Baby, smudge-faced, wild-haired, staggers in upstage right behind the others, in a singed beard and what's left of a Santa suit: Christmas boxer shorts, one ragged boot, his jacket missing a sleeve.)*

BABY. *(Rambles, crazed.)* Santa Ana…wrong Santa…Santa Ana… Bad Santa! *(Staggers out upstage left, Sloggett races after him.)*

LARK. *(To camera.)* That's right. We're a vital community, involved in regular county-wide events.

GEORGIA DEAN. Doublewide is the new hometown for you. It's where people genuinely care for one another. *(SFX: Gunshot! Patsy screams, sprints in stage left in front of the others, exits stage right. Big Ethel races in stage left.)*

BIG ETHEL. Bob and weave all you want, heifer! I've got all day! *(Runs off stage right.)*

JOVEETA. *(Doggedly to camera.)* Wake up every morning in the beautiful Texas countryside. Ours is a community where you can live in perfect harmony with nature. *(Just then, Baby runs in stage right behind the others, screams, wrestles with a raccoon attached to his head. Sloggett, on his heels, tries to help.)*

SLOGGETT. It's revenge, Baby! Those raccoons are getting even for Davy Crockett's coonskin cap! *(Baby, Sloggett fight raccoon as they exit stage right.)*

LARK. *(Determined, to camera.)* Every time you hear the words *Doublewide, Texas*, we want you to think "What an opportunity!" *(Caprice hurries in stage right, her face smudge free.)*

CAPRICE. *(Stands in front of Joveeta. To camera.)* And speaking of great opportunities, it is I, back to deliver a special Christmas message in song. *(Sings to the tune of "O Little Town of Bethlehem.")*
    O LITTLE TOWN OF DOUBLEWIDE
    THE SWEETEST IN THE STATE…

JOVEETA. *(Desperate, to camera.)* Well, thank you so much for that information, colorful resident. *(Painfully gets to her feet.)* I'm sure everyone watching can see living in Doublewide is a unique experience you can't find anywhere else. *(Steps in front of Caprice.)*

CAPRICE. *(Undaunted, leans out from behind Joveeta, continues to sing.)*
    COME CHANGE YOUR LIFE
    GIVE UP YOUR STRIFE
    BEFORE IT'S ALL TOO LATE…

JOVEETA. Just contact us here at— *(Patsy yells, runs in stage right in front of Joveeta and Caprice, Big Ethel barrels in stage right. Patsy grabs Georgia Dean as a human shield. Joveeta, with increasing urgency, speaks louder.)* Go to your phones now and make a simple call that will improve your life. Just dial— *(Baby screams, runs in stage left behind the women, a raccoon on his head, a second one clamped onto his behind. Sloggett puffs in stage left, gets to Baby, struggles with the raccoons. Baby races off stage right.)*

CAPRICE. *(Leans out from Joveeta's other side, sings.)*
    ENJOY A DOSE OF FREEDOM
    WITH A CELEBRITY—

JOVEETA. *(Throws up her hands, defeated, roars.)* THAT DOES IT! EVERYONE JUST STOP! *(They do and slowly move toward her.*

Joveeta forgets "the camera," addresses the others.) Unbelievable! Can't you people pull it together? We only have one chance to save this town and— *(Checks watch, deflates.)* we failed. *(Sighs.)* We're out of time. We blew it. We were just *live* on television. *(The others are confused, worried.)* But instead of selling viewers on how wonderful our little town is and what a happy life we have here, we acted like crazy people—caterwauling, waving guns around, fighting wild animals—and wasting our *five precious minutes!* So, it's over. Our big chance. Any dream we had of keeping Doublewide alive…is over. We came so close. *(Sighs.)* Everyone just…go home. *(Rubs her back, limps off stage right. Long beat. The others look at each other, guilty.)*

BIG ETHEL. How come Joveeta didn't tell us we were on the TV?

SLOGGETT. Because she was afraid what just happened *would* happen. *(Defeated.)* And she was right. We blew it.

BIG ETHEL. Okay, folks, this is how it is. We've embarrassed ourselves in front of the entire county—

CAPRICE. Thanks to Patsy.

BIG ETHEL. We've humiliated ourselves in front of half the State—

CAPRICE. Okay, that one's on us.

BIG ETHEL. Our town is done for, y'all. There's no goin' back. *(Beat. They take it in. Baby staggers in stage right.)*

BABY. *(Shouts.)* Did you know there was an explosion at the competition? I was right by it and can't hear nothin' except all this ringin'!

GEORGIA DEAN. This is awful. And it's Arden Rose's first Christmas.

BIG ETHEL. All I can say is, it's been a privilege and an adventure livin' next door to you people. *(Puts her arm around Georgia Dean, they exit stage right.)*

CAPRICE. *(Takes Baby by the arm. Shouts.)* Let's get you out of that costume, Baby, then pop a top and see what we've got to eat besides yams and C-Rations.

BABY. *(Shouts.)* I wish someone would answer that phone. It won't stop ringin'! *(They exit. Beat.)*

PATSY. *(Flippant.)* Oh well, all good things must come to an end. I'm going home. *(Starts to exit stage right.)*

SLOGGETT. *(Deadly.)* Freeze right there, hell cat. *(Shocked, she does *so. He advances on her slowly, deliberately.*) I told you how the good people in this little town gave me a second chance. You could've had that, too, but you gave it all up for your sour revenge. You've lost your chance, Patsy, and thanks to you, we all have, too. I honestly believe you're incapable of doing anything for anyone but yourself. And now you've ruined our Christmas. I don't know what's going to happen to you and frankly, I really don't care. *(Exits stage left. Long beat.)*

PATSY. *(To Lark. Tentative.)* I guess you hate me, too.

LARK. *(Crosses to her.)* Of course not. I couldn't hate you. You're my Great-Aunt Patsy. I *am* disappointed in you but I love you. Everyone deserves to be loved, especially at Christmas. *(Surprises Patsy by taking her hand.)*

PATSY. *(Touched, sighs.)* I've made a fine mess of things, haven't I?

LARK. *(Gentle.)* Know what? I believe there's always another chance if you just look for it. *(Patsy pats the baby's head, starts off stage left.)* But if I were you… *(Patsy stops, turns back. Then Lark, feisty.)* I'd start by kissing butts around here *as fast as I could, so get to it!* *(Patsy hurries off stage left. Lark kisses the baby. Then.)* Arden Rose, I've got a real strong vibe about this—maybe I really *am* becoming a Texan because I'm not giving up hope. Bad as things look right now, I still believe something awesome could come from all this. *(Joveeta limps in stage left to get her ball, her hand on her back.)*

JOVEETA. *(End of her rope.)* I just want to crawl into a hole. Worst. Christmas Eve. Ever. It can't get any—

HARLEY. *(Voiceover.)* And that does it from the little town of Doublewide. Thank you for watching Totally Texas Television! *(Joveeta and Lark's heads whip toward the camera, deer in the headlights.)* Annnnd, we're off!

LARK. You mean we've been on the air this entire—

HARLEY. *(Voiceover.)* Sure have! Boy howdy, I bet half the State just witnessed that hot mess. Well, Merry Christmas, y'all! That's a wrap! *(Frozen in horror, Joveeta and Lark stare out at the audience, look at one another, back out at the audience. Joveeta lets out a little tiny scream. Blackout.)*

Scene 6

The next night. Lights come up on Joveeta's living room. Joveeta, dejected, in jeans and a sweatshirt, cleans out her desk, puts documents, keepsakes into a box. The croquet mallet sticks up out of the box. She picks up the little gavel, studies it. Georgia Dean, in another Christmas sweater, enters from kitchen with two mugs.

GEORGIA DEAN. Hope you're hungry. Everyone's cooking up a storm and this potluck Christmas dinner is shaping up to be one heck of a final wing-ding. When O.C. was emptying their freezer, he found something petrified he thinks might've started out as venison. He took it out back and threw it on the grill.

JOVEETA. I'm sure going to miss this place. But, hey, we all tried our best.

GEORGIA DEAN. Nothing's written in stone yet. Something wonderful could still happen. So put that gavel down and drink up. *(Hands her a mug, they toast.)*

JOVEETA. *(Sips.)* Yeah, there'll be plenty of time tomorrow to— Whoa! This has some kind of kick! I think my back just popped into place. What's in this?

GEORGIA DEAN. Mucho tequila! It's my Huevo Nog—a brand new Lone Star tradition! After all we've been through, we deserve this. *(They sip as Lark and Arden Rose enter from kitchen.)*

LARK. Anyone know if Great-Aunt Patsy's going to show up for supper? Or ever again?

GEORGIA DEAN. Nobody's seen her since last night. It's pitiful she's made herself an outcast, but it's her own fault.

LARK. Oh, I totally forgot! Earlcody stopped by this morning and left this for you. *(Pulls an envelope from her pocket.)*

GEORGIA DEAN. How sweet. Maybe it's a Christmas bonus, but he— *(Opens it, scans it, screams.)* Oh, my God!

LARK. Did I bring you bad news?

GEORGIA DEAN. No, no! *(Reads.)* Earlcody says when the fire-works went off at the Nativity Smackdown, mortality tapped him on the shoulder. He realized it was time to take a heart pill *and* give me the Buffeteria! And he did! This is a deed of sale for *one dollar*! It means *I'm the new Bronco Betty*! *(They squeal, delighted.)*

JOVEETA. Maybe we can all move into the Buffeteria! I'll take the storeroom!

GEORGIA DEAN. See, this is what I was talking about, Joveeta! And now something good *has* happened. *(To Arden Rose.)* Isn't that exciting, little girl? *(Whispers.)* Geor-gia Dean, Geor-gia Dean.

LARK. She's excited alright. And she's got the wet diaper to prove it. Be right back. *(Races out hallway door. Caprice enters from kitchen with a beer.)*

JOVEETA. Hey, Jingle Belle, want to hear some great news?!

CAPRICE. *(Grumpy.)* Not as much as I want to drink this beer. My wagon's dragging. I had lousy dreams last night.

JOVEETA. What kind? Murder, kidnapping, not being asked for your autograph at the Dairy Dog drive-thru, what?

CAPRICE. Even worse... *(Low.)* this very *suggestive* dream about— about *getting frisky* with—I can't even say the name. *(Sloggett enters from hallway door.)*

SLOGGETT. Well, looky here. *(Moves to Caprice with a sexy, hip-swiveling swagger.)* Hey, Caprice! Or should I call you *dream girl*? Disappointed to see me... *(Sexy.)* wearing pants?

CAPRICE. *(Wheels on Georgia Dean.)* Traitor! You swore you wouldn't tell!

GEORGIA DEAN. Actually, it only seemed fair to level the playing field.

JOVEETA. Hold on. Not that you want *my* opinion, *Mama,*—now or *ever*—but is there a chance these dreams you two are having might really have a *deeper meaning*?

CAPRICE/SLOGGETT. *(They look at each other. Then, defensive.)* Oh, no!/Hell, no! *(Baby races in hallway door, carries blankets and a bag of dog food.)*

BABY. Georgia Dean, I'm makin' a Christmas truce with your

raccoons. See? I'm gettin' to play Santa after all! I'm turnin' that old pickup out front into their own critter condo and they're lovin' it. We can tow it behind our trailer when we leave.

GEORGIA DEAN. I'm not sure you had to go that far to make nice with them.

BABY. Uh, yeah, I did, unless I want to sleep with one eye open the rest of my life. They let me off the hook for hasslin' 'em, just like y'all let me off the hook for cookin' up and eatin' Lady Bird. *(Runs out front door. Big Ethel bursts through the kitchen door, phone in one hand, a yam in the other.)*

BIG ETHEL. Y'all will *never* believe what I've got to tell you!

GEORGIA DEAN. If it's bad news, just hold your horses. We're all gonna need some of my Huevo Nog to make it go down easier. *(Lark enters from hallway door without Arden Rose. Big Ethel puts the yam on the dining table.)*

BIG ETHEL. We're gonna need a glass of somethin' alright...*to celebrate!* Cee Cee just called. *We won the Battle of the Mangers! (Shock! Then cheers, hugs.)* She said our display was patriotic and imaginative and the *fireworks put it over the top.* All the judges appreciated that *Nativity at the Alamo* was the only *interactive entry* in the bunch. In spite of it bein' a little scary, everyone *loved* it! *(More cheers, hugs. Sloggett and Caprice inadvertently give each other a bear hug, realize it, quickly separate.)* Now nobody can pretend we're not just as good as any other town in McTwayne County! *(Beat. Reality hits.)*

SLOGGETT. Too bad after next week we won't even exist anymore. *(Everyone's bummed. Beat.)*

JOVEETA. The heck with it! *We won! (They all cheer, hug again as Patsy enters hallway door.)*

PATSY. *(Humble.)* Okay if I come in? *(Everyone stops.)*

CAPRICE. Boy, talk about a *buzz kill.*

PATSY. I know I've got some nerve showing my face here tonight.

SLOGGETT. Pretty much what *I'm* thinking. *(The others mutter agreement.)*

LARK. Everyone in this room knows what Aunt Patsy did was

wrong. But if she hadn't snuck in the fireworks, we wouldn't have won the contest. And there's no denying that. *(Beat. They mull it over.)*

JOVEETA. Personally, I'd still like to deny it a little bit.

PATSY. Oh, so you already heard. Tina Jo called to tell me…and to thank me for making the competition such a big hit. First kind words she's offered in years.

BIG ETHEL. Did you tell her you really meant to blow the whole thing up?

PATSY. Hey, I may be petty and vengeful, but I'm not *stupid*. *(Steadies herself.)* Haywood, I haven't stopped thinking about what you and Lark said to me last night and…I realized I wasn't just facing Christmas alone, but the rest of my life as well. And that kind of reckoning drop-kicks you right back into reality. I was handed a second chance and threw it away. I'm so very, very sorry for dragging y'all into my plan for revenge. I went way too far and I honestly want to wipe the slate clean…and I hope you'll let me. *(Nobody responds.)* Well, I don't really blame you, I should probably go. *(Starts to exit hallway door.)*

LARK. Wait! *I* will, Aunt Patsy. *(Nudges Georgia Dean.)*

GEORGIA DEAN. *(Gives in.)* Okay. I will, too. *(Gives Joveeta a look.)*

JOVEETA. *(With difficulty.)* Fine. Me, too.

SLOGGETT. Yeah, we all will.

CAPRICE. Not me! Am I the only person in this room with a backbone?!

LARK. Caprice, it's Christmas. She apologized and did I mention it's *Christmas*?

CAPRICE. Okay, I give. But I reserve the right to bear a grudge.

BIG ETHEL. *(Reluctant.)* And Patsy, you should…stay for Christmas supper…but you oughta know, my rifle's still loaded.

PATSY. Is that okay with you, Haywood? *(Sloggett nods.)* Great. Then I should tell you I've brought a guest. *(Goes to front door.)*

JOVEETA. You know, Patsy, there *is* a fine line between forgiveness and pushing your luck. *(Patsy opens front door. A rugged outdoorsman in a Santa hat and beard, sunglasses, colorful Hawaiian shirt, shorts and a backpack enters. It's Nash Sloggett. Instrumental version of "The First Noel" comes up softly.)*

NASH. Ho, ho, ho! Merry Christmas! *(The others are confused. He takes off his sunglasses, pulls off his beard.)*

GEORGIA DEAN. *(Stunned.)* Nash?!

NASH. *(Smiles.)* Hello, beautiful. *(They move to each other, kiss, embrace. Sloggett steps back, too stunned to speak.)*

CAPRICE. Dang it, Joveeta, if you'd just used that dating service, this could've been you. *(Patsy crosses to them, taps Nash on the shoulder. He turns to her.)*

PATSY. Sorry to interrupt, Nash. But there's someone you need to meet. *(Pulls Lark to him.)* This is Lark, your daughter. *(They stare at each other a beat.)*

NASH. I'm so sorry but I never knew that you—

LARK. It's okay. I know. My mom told me.

NASH. You look just like her. *(They embrace as Georgia Dean moves to Sloggett, puts her arm around him. Joveeta goes to Patsy.)*

JOVEETA. *(Low.)* How on earth did you find him when no one else could?

PATSY. I've always tried to have some idea of where that boy was. You know, in case I needed a bone marrow donor or something. *(Big Ethel joins them.)* I found him in Hawaii. He takes people deep sea fishing. I caught him between charters.

BIG ETHEL. I've always prided myself on bein' a *get 'er done gal*, but if you pulled this off in twenty-four hours, you leave me in the dust, woman.

PATSY. It wasn't easy, but when I finally got hold of him, I told Nash he needed to come home. Actually, he said he'd been thinking about it for a while. And he was ready. *(Georgia Dean gently pushes Sloggett toward Nash.)*

SLOGGETT. *(Apprehensive.)* Hello, son.

NASH. *(Turns to Sloggett. Beat.)* Hi, Dad. Um…this was all fairly short notice. I didn't have time to get you a gift or anything. I'm sorry.

SLOGGETT. It's okay. There's only one thing I want for Christmas.

NASH. What's that?

SLOGGETT. *(Hard for him to say.)* Forgiveness.

NASH. *(Kind.)* You're in luck. I brought a whole lot of that with me. *(They embrace, a bear hug. Thrilled, Georgia Dean and Lark put their arms around each other, watch Nash and his dad. Caprice saunters to the sofa.)*

CAPRICE. You know, Patsy, under that surly attitude and all them stuck-up airs, you may actually have a heart. That's right commendable. 'Course it's not as good as being *famous* like me, but it'll do. *(Plops down on the end of the sofa.)*

PATSY. Well, when you screw up big, you have to make it up *bigger*. Besides, Haywood gave me a second chance, the least I could do was return the favor. *(Sits in middle of the sofa, falls down into the dip. Caprice stares down at her.)* You know, you could've reminded me of this.

CAPRICE. Yeah, I coulda…but I'm not there yet. *(Lark races out hallway door as Big Ethel hurries over to help Patsy up. Joveeta crosses to Nash.)*

JOVEETA. Welcome home, Nash, you've been missed. We're glad you're here.

NASH. Thanks, Joveeta. *(As he talks, he absent-mindedly picks up the yam, toys with it.)* It's been a long time, but— *(Stops, re: yam.)* Wow! This thing looks exactly like Willie Nelson!

BIG ETHEL. *(Runs to him, grabs the yam.)* Holy cats! We've got us another winner! *(To the others.)* This boy may have lived in Hi-wah-yah, but he's still got plenty of Texas in him! *(Claps Nash on the back. Lark enters hallway door, Arden Rose, wrapped in a blanket, in her arms.)*

LARK. Hey, I've got a sleepyhead here who'd like to meet her grandfather. *(Puts Arden Rose in his arms. Nash is overwhelmed. Beat.)*

NASH. I've got to say, everything I could ever want is right here— my dad, a daughter and baby granddaughter and the love of my life. All this on top of jet lag is a lot to take in. *(Beat.)* Somebody say something. *(Beat of silence. SFX: A baby voice says "Pat-sy!" The group turns to Arden Rose. SFX: "Pat-sy!" They gasp.)*

JOVEETA. Hold it! She just said her first word and it was—

GEORGIA DEAN. *Patsy?!* I've been whispering *my* name to her for months!

PATSY. *(Thrilled, rushes to Arden Rose.)* This baby's a genius! Guess she takes after her Great-Great-Aunt. *(Coos to the baby.)* Yes, she does. She's a little smarty.

CAPRICE. If Patsy's through rubbing our noses in it, what say we all sit down to Christmas supper? Come on, Nash, we've got more food than we can handle.

NASH. I figured. You're going to need it with all those people you invited.

JOVEETA. What are you talking about?

NASH. All those folks waiting out front. There must be forty or fifty of them. Y'all sure have a lot of friends. *(Baby bursts in front door.)*

BABY. Hey, we got people outside who've come here from everywhere in Texas! They all saw the show on TV last night.

JOVEETA. *(Cringes.)* Great. So they all saw us make fools of ourselves. They're probably here to see for themselves what kind of idiots live in Doublewide.

BABY. Nothin' like that. They're real nice. We was visitin' and most of 'em told me they thought our Christmas Eve show was *a hoot.* They say Doublewide looks like a fun place to live and *they all want to move here now*! *(Everyone's stunned.)*

SLOGGETT. That's…that's incredible! I can't believe it!

BIG ETHEL. *(Looks out the window.)* Holy cow, look how many are out there! *(Caprice and Sloggett join her.)*

CAPRICE. I *knew* living next to me would be the big draw! We're not gonna just *double* Doublewide, we're going to *quadruple* it!

BABY. And the first guy in line is Boyce Buttram, Loydene's son! Me and him was in 4-H together and he says he and his family are callin' "dibs" on the space next to me and Mama. *(Hands Joveeta a manila envelope.)* Oh, he says Loydene wants you to have this. She says "you win."

JOVEETA. *(Rips it open, pulls out letters.)* Oh, my gosh! These are the certified incorporation papers! We're *official*, y'all! They can't

59

ever take it away from us now! *(Cheers, hugs as Joveeta studies the letters.)* Wait! We've also gotten four of the grants we applied for! We can start upgrading our town! *(Cheers.)* We did it!

LARK. We just proved it's still possible for the little guys to beat the big guys!

CAPRICE. Hell, girl, this is Texas! *Anything's* possible!

BABY. Yeah, look at me. I finally got to play Santa!

BIG ETHEL. Now let's go out and welcome our new neighbors! *(She and Baby rush out front door as Nash hands Arden Rose to Lark.)*

GEORGIA DEAN. See, I told y'all not to give up.

LARK. *(Beams at Nash.)* I never did.

NASH. Well, if I'm going to live here, guess I need to meet those folks, too. *(To Georgia Dean.)* Want to go with me? *(She hurries to him, takes his hand.)*

GEORGIA DEAN. *(Big smile.)* Always have, always will. *(They start for front door.)* Hey, Caprice, Sloggett! Don't forget the mistletoe. *(Points to it, teases.)* Shame not to make good use of it. *(She and Nash kiss, exit. Caprice and Sloggett look at each other, horrified. He speeds to the desk, grabs croquet mallet, yanks the mistletoe down, throws it on the floor behind the couch, pounds it repeatedly.)*

CAPRICE. 'Atta boy! Smack it again! Harder! *(He stands, all smiles, throws the mallet down, satisfied.)* Yeah, we killed that sucker! Way to go, Sloggett.

SLOGGETT. Consider it my Christmas gift, Crumpler. Now, come on, let's go put out the welcome mat. *(They start for the door, Caprice turns back, stomps the mistletoe one last time. They exit front door.)*

PATSY. After all we've gone through, how on earth did it all turn out so well?

LARK. *(Takes her hand.)* Guess that's just the magic of Christmas. *(They exit front door. Joveeta hurries to the box next to the desk. SFX: "Jingle Bells" comes up softly. She pulls out the gavel.)*

JOVEETA. *(Checks to see she's alone. Then, as if in a meeting.)* As Mayor of this newly incorporated town, I hereby declare that

Doublewide, Texas is open for business—on this, *the very best Christmas ever! (SFX: Music comes up full! She hammers the gavel twice, kisses the papers, throws her arms victoriously in the air. Her back goes out. She grabs it.)* Ow! Ow! Ow! *(Blackout.)*

End of Play

PROPERTY LIST

Flashlight
Cell phones
Lifelike doll in snuggly
Strings of Christmas lights
Large plastic Nativity figure
Sheaf of papers
Beer bottles
Gift card and envelope
Makeup bottle
Folding chairs
Rope
Life-size plush toy raccoons
Small gavel and sound block
Croquet mallet
Shopping bag
Coat
Negligee
Hand mixer missing one beater
Tray of dessert bars
Bushel basket of sweet potatoes
Large exercise ball
Small candy cane
Roll of electrical tape
Paper currency
Woman's wig
Battery-powered drill
Stack of printed flyers
Plates
Forks and spoons
Small decorated Christmas tree
Oven mitts
Sweet potato casserole in baking dish
Large sign framed in tinsel
Man's Western hat
Flask
Small cosmetic bag
Comb

Face powder
Hand-lettered signs
Rifle
Assorted desk items—documents, stapler, etc.
Cardboard box
Coffee mugs
White business envelope and letter
Blankets
Bag of dry dog food
Sunglasses
Backpack
Manila envelope with letters inside
Bunch of mistletoe

SOUND EFFECTS

Loud electrical buzz

Cell phone ringing

Sounds of laughter and glasses clinking

Sounds of raccoons growling, screeching, chattering

Lively instrumental version of "Jingle Bells"

Rifle shot

Instrumental version of "The First Noel"

A baby's voice

Soft instrumental version of "Jingle Bells"

Note on Songs/Recordings, Images, or Other Production Design Elements

Be advised that Dramatists Play Service, Inc., neither holds the rights to nor grants permission to use any songs, recordings, images, or other design elements mentioned in the play. Jones Hope Wooten do not use copyrighted material in their plays. Any songs written into Jones Hope Wooten plays must be performed exactly as written, including but not limited to the indicated melody and the staging of such songs. No other songs, recordings, or production elements may be incorporated or substituted for specific elements written into the play.

If any copyrighted material is used in a production of a Jones Hope Wooten play, including but not limited to pre-show music, it is the responsibility of the producing theater/organization to obtain permission of the copyright owner(s) for any such use. Additional royalty fees may apply for the right to use copyrighted materials. Dramatists Play Service, Inc., does not assist in clearing rights to materials not specifically written into acting editions. DPS cannot advise as to whether or not a song/arrangement/recording, image, or other design element is in the public domain.